GHOSTS
OF THE
RICH
AND
FAMOUS

GHOSTS OF THE RICH AND FAMOUS

ARTHUR MYERS

CB
CONTEMPORARY
BOOKS
CHICAGO · NEW YORK

Library of Congress Cataloging-in-Publication Data

Myers, Arthur.
    Ghosts of the rich and famous / Arthur Myers.
        p.   cm.
    Includes index.
    ISBN 0-8092-4647-3 : $9.95
        1. Ghosts.   2. Celebrities—Miscellanea.   I. Title.
    BF1471.M96   1988
    133.1—dc19   88-22751
                                                                    CIP

A James Peter Book
James Peter Associates, Inc.

Published by Contemporary Books, Inc.
180 North Michigan Avenue, Chicago, Illinois 60601
Manufactured in the United States of America
International Standard Book Number: 0-8092-4647-3

Published simultaneously in Canada by Beaverbooks, Ltd.
195 Allstate Parkway, Valleywood Business Park
Markham, Ontario L3R 4T8 Canada

*This book is dedicated
to Virginia Ritchie Cutler,
its first reader.*

CONTENTS

GHOSTS OF THE RICH AND FAMOUS

INTRODUCTION:
Adventures of an Author on His Journey to the Final Page

I used to wonder why authors wrote introductions to their books.

Does anybody read them? I certainly don't. If I'm going to read a book, I plunge right in. Usually somewhere in the middle.

But now that I write books myself, I can see why authors write introductions, self-indulgent though it may be.

When I was a newspaperman, I once had a sympathetic city editor, a rare strain of that life form. If the piece you had slaved over all that morning didn't make it into the paper, he would sidle up to your desk and murmur apologetically, "Sorry, but your story fell outside the breastworks." It was a rather charming way of putting it; kind of old-fashioned, even fusty. I think he was a Civil War buff.

Anyway, it's the same with a book. Even though a

1

book author is to a certain extent his own editor, he can't fit in everything. And every author feels there is so much he wanted to say that didn't quite make it, so much fascinating, astonishing, exciting, arcane material that for one reason or another fell outside the breastworks.

Of course, nobody else gives a hoot. But authors don't know that. All they know is that they are determined to make one last desperate lunge at getting that stuff in.

That's why introductions were born, and here is the introduction to this book.

Marilyn Monroe, John Lennon, Elvis Presley, Johann Sebastian Bach, Harry Houdini, Admiral Richard E. Byrd—many dearly departed celebrities seem to need to communicate to those of us on earth. Whether it's returning as an apparition, responding to a séance, placing their voices on blank tape, speaking to us through a channeler, or any of a variety of paranormal phenomena, these and many other well-known ghosts are purported to be among us, and their stories are told here.

Sometimes the *witness* is the celebrity—and very much alive—be it Elke Sommer, Jimmy Carter, or Allen Ginsberg. Their stories are here, too.

I selected the ghost stories in this volume based on the wealth or fame (or both) of the ghosts or their witnesses; the ability of the reported occurrence to startle the reader, or at least to make him or her think twice about the paranormal; and the credibility of the story.

As for the latter consideration, I have usually kept to stories that have some degree of what parapsychologists call *evidentiality*—which means that there is strong evidence that what is purported to be true is in fact true.

The first psychic I met repeatedly called me back within thirty seconds after I had called her and found her line busy; those are evidential psychic powers at work. On first meeting me, she told me a specific detail about my life she could not have known by normal means; that's evidential. She could predict the future pretty well, too; that's very evidential.

Most of us have not had the fortune—good or bad— to be around when a ghost walks, but if a trustworthy person says it happened to him or her, that's evidential to a degree.

For example, a very practical, sensible, and eminently trustworthy eighty-three-year-old man I know, Ted Coleman, wrote me with this story. Coleman retired as a vice president of Northrop Corporation, the aircraft manufacturer. For a retirement job, he became city manager of South Pasadena, California. Not long after he and his family moved into a house in Pasadena that had originally been owned by a well-known doctor named Sam Madison, Ted's wife and the Coleman's maid began to believe the place was haunted. His wife claimed the cushions on their bedroom chairs would suddenly depress, as if someone were sitting against them, and then would expand after a few minutes, as though the invisible person had gotten up. The maid insisted that Sam Madison's ghost constantly got into her path as she swept the upstairs hallway, and it got to the point where she refused to go upstairs alone.

Down-to-earth Ted took all this with a block of salt

until one day, as he wrote: "Without warning, the curtains suspended from rings in the rods over the windows in the den where I would be working would suddenly, without warning, slide to one side on their rings and open up a gap, exposing the open window. When I would rise to investigate, the curtains would suddenly move back into place and close the gap before I could reach them."

That's evidential.

I always try to get corroboration for any stories that come my way, for if a story hangs completely on the subjective experience of one person, it has very little evidentiality. I have shied away from this sort of thing—although occasionally I have included one that is too entertaining to pass up.

To help the reader decide on the evidentiality of each story, I have made clear its source or sources. I've identified source publications and have tried to give some idea of the background, character, or reputation of people who were sources.

When a friend of mine heard I was writing about celebrities and ghosts, he gave me a book titled *The Curse of Macbeth*. Written by Richard Huggett, an English actor, it is a very entertaining read, although not too helpful for my purposes. Most of the stories involve English actors little known on this side of the Atlantic. But there was one delightful anecdote, which I reproduce here verbatim:

"Sir Alec Guinness was supposed to have seen the ghost of Shakespeare sitting in the stalls on the first night of his ill-starred 1951 *Hamlet* who supposedly got up and walked out in the middle of the performance. The press played this story up in a big way and it has since appeared in magazines and books dealing with the occult. I wrote to Sir Alec for confirmation and discovered from him that the whole story rose from a little misunderstanding. What he said to his fellow actor in the interval was not that he had seen Shakespeare get up and leave but that he had seen somebody *looking* like Shakespeare. The mysterious stranger turned out to be Somerset Maugham.''

The British royal family has been known for generations to be composed of psychic buffs. The present Queen Mother is reputed to have seen a psychic regularly, and Prince Charles, who seems somewhat of a New Age type anyway, also is said to dabble in these things.

Possibly the best-known English royal devotee of the psychic was Queen Victoria. She became particularly involved after the death of her husband, Prince Albert. She had her own private medium, a Scottish servant named John Brown, to whom she became quite devoted.

When Benjamin Disraeli, the flamboyant prime minister of her day, was on his deathbed, she offered to pay him a visit.

"No," Disraeli is reputed to have said, "it is better not. She will only ask me to take a message to Albert."

While perusing one of the supermarket tabloids one day I came across a story that claimed that apparitions of John Wayne have been spotted at both the Alamo and the White House. Agog, I phoned the Alamo, but

authorities there said this was news to them. I decided
to pass on the White House, but if Ronnie Reagan
could make it to the White House, I wouldn't be surprised to find the Duke floating around there, too.

I got to thinking, *American Heritage* ought to have a
ghost or two among all its chronicles—some good
historical spooks. The magazine might be a real trea-
sure trove. So I went to the library and got out its index.
There was only one promising entry, "Ghosts in the
White House." I looked it up. Turned out they were
talking about ghost*writers*.

One pitfall of researching a book like this is that a
lot of ghosts are touted as celebrities but turn out to be
merely the spirits of one-time janitors still nosing
about the place or somebody who lived down the block.
While vacationing in historic Newport, Rhode Island,
I kept hearing about the great ghosts they had in
town—specifically those of Henry James, Benjamin
Franklin, and the famed early American naval officer
Stephen Decatur.

James was supposedly haunting a house he had lived
in as a boy. Franklin was purportedly hanging about
the Franklin Printing House, founded by his brother
James in 1727, and where Ben worked briefly in his
youth. Decatur is rumored to be wandering up and
down the waterfront.

These are worth checking out, I said to myself, and,
between buying postcards, betting on jai alai, and
wolfing down seafood, I started making phone calls.

I put in a call to the Franklin Printing House and
spoke with the proprietor, Aaron Slom. "We used to be

at 183 Thames Street," Slom said, "and we used to work late at night. There was much ado by many of my employees. My foreman, Glenn Bissell, used to talk about it a lot—footsteps and so on. I heard something banging around myself. The place burned down a few years ago. We called the ghost Ben."

"But how do you know it was Ben Franklin?"

The rationale was that Ben once worked there, so *maybe* it was him. My own theory is that it was an old printer trying to find a Linotype machine among all the computers.

So I turned to Henry James, said by Newporters to be haunting the O'Neill-Hayes Funeral Home. I phoned the funeral home and got Charlie Hayes, the fifth generation of Hayeses to live in the place. Charlie said he wasn't psychic but his wife, Patty, was. She told me of sensing a presence, feeling unaccountable drafts, seeing a blur go by, and smelling perfume. Sure sounds like a ghost, I thought, but more like a female ghost. Unless Henry James used perfume—which, of course, is possible.

I called Charlie's father, John, in Florida, and he confirmed that the funeral home had been a house in which the Jameses had lived when Henry was a child. John said he had never seen or heard anything but gave me the phone number of another of his sons, Joe, who had had a paranormal experience in the house some years before.

Joe was quite forthcoming. "I was a teenager," he told me. "I was sleeping in a room with two of my younger brothers. I awoke one night and saw what I took to be a woman. The figure appeared to be floating a few inches off the floor. It sort of hovered over my brother. I was pretty scared. The figure disappeared and I woke my brother, who wasn't aware of anything."

"But no Henry James?" I asked.

No, just the woman, he replied, and he saw her only once.

Sounds like the wrong ghost to me.

I decided to forget about Decatur. He may be wandering up and down the Newport waterfront among the bistros and boutiques, but you can't prove it by me.

One of the most pertinent comments on parapsychology that I've heard came from Boyce Batey, a New England parapsychologist. When I first met Batey, he seemed most reserved, sober, seemingly humorless. Parapsychologists do tend to come on as slide rule types, as statisticians. Batey *is* in fact a statistician employed by a Hartford insurance company. After two or three hours in his company I wasn't expecting any belly laughs. As we were breaking up, I cast about for something perspicacious to say and came up with, "Well, I guess a parapsychologist has to keep an open mind."

"Yes," Boyce said, "but in this whole field you have to tread a narrow path between having an open mind and a hole in the head."

And before we get into the book proper, how about a little poetry about ghosts? Here is a spooky poem by a friend of mine, Margaret Kay of Allston, Massachusetts:

Two Ghosts

Well, you surprised me. I
didn't expect to find you here
on this rickety pier, feet
dangling beside the moss-slippery
wharf ladder, looking out
at the cold sea.

I looked for you in the cemetery,
but you weren't there. So I
straightened the flag on your
great-grandfather's grave and sat and
watched the mail boat chopping its way
over the grey water toward Cherry Island.
Then I came and found you here.

What am I doing here? If you
must know, I'm watching that old
herring gull wine and dine his wife
with the sweet-tasting mud shrimps he
finds under the rocks. Any law against
that? Do you have your own
exclusive name on this whole Island?

Herring gulls mate for life, did
you know that, you expert on
things of the sea? Listen to her

gurgle her low throaty gurgle.
She knows a good thing when she
sees one. She doesn't need to go
looking for someone else to love.

Yes. Yes, I can see the fog
rolling in from Grand Manan. Don't
worry, I'll be going soon. Then you
can have this pebbly beach all to
yourself. I'm going to a warm and
sandy beach, where palms sway and surf
breaks against white sand. I'll
sit in a bar and listen to the
soft clink of glasses and drink
Bloody Marys and eat grouper and
stone crabs. Remember?

I
THE MOVIES

1
ARE GABLE AND LOMBARD HAUNTING THIS LITTLE HOTEL IN ARIZONA?

Preparing a book that deals with famous people involves different problems than does one concerning ordinary, down-the-street ghosts. In my previous book, *The Ghostly Register,* I took the ghosts as I found them; very few of the people I interviewed had anything to gain by falsifying information. But people cluster around celebrities and many would love to be mentioned in a book as having had a relationship, albeit posthumous, with one of the rich and famous. So one must be wary.

For example, while I was working on a prospective chapter about Frances Farmer and her apparent postmortem activities in Indianapolis, where she spent her last years, a highly regarded psychic I know advised me against contacting certain people. "They'd have stories to tell, I'm sure," she said. "A lot of people want notoriety. Frances has been manipulated in death as well as in life.''

I decided to scratch the chapter on Frances Farmer.

A researcher must treat information from the media carefully, too. Much that appears in newspapers or goes out over the air is a bit inaccurate, to say the least. Having been interviewed a number of times myself, I am bemused at how seldom reporters get the story completely right, or create distortion by accident. But some reporters create distortion on purpose. One finds the latter particularly in the supermarket tabloids. For example, consider the following headline:

GABLE AND LOMBARD: THEIR HAUNTING
LOVE—GHOSTS OF INSEPARABLE LOVERS STALK
HONEYMOON HOTEL

Or this one:

GHOSTS OF GABLE & LOMBARD HAUNT HOTEL

Newspapers rewrite each other with wild abandon; it's one of the folkways of journalism. The stories in both papers are essentially the same. A researcher will find a slight glitch in the premise of each of these stories: that these star-crossed lovers are hanging out to this day—and night—in the Oatman Hotel in Oatman, Arizona.

Let's start with a few incontrovertible facts: Oatman is a village of about 150 permanent residents; it is located some 30 miles from the Nevada border, 120 miles south of Las Vegas and 300 miles from Los Angeles. Once a gold-mining town, it is now something of a tourist attraction. Some film companies use the area for location work since it is in the mountains and near the Colorado River. One longtime resident says, "Howard Hughes and Jeff Chandler were here when they were making *Foxfire*; Debbie Reynolds was here when they were doing some of the filming of *How the West Was Won*."

The Oatman Hotel is a two-story building. The second floor is now used as a museum of the old gold-mining days; the sixteen rooms are separated from the corridor by screens. One, the Theater Room, contains an old movie projector, old posters, and water buckets and tin cups that predate the invention of the lobby bubbler.

Clark Gable and Carole Lombard were married on March 29, 1939, in Kingman, Arizona, a piece up the road from Oatman on old Route 66. They then headed for Los Angeles but spent at least their wedding night at the Oatman Hotel. Lombard died in an air crash in the Rocky Mountains in 1942; Gable died of a heart attack in 1960.

After contacting three people mentioned in the newspaper stories about the Oatman Hotel, I found that it certainly does seem to be haunted. It is highly unlikely that Gable and Lombard are the haunters, however.

According to the stories, many eerie things happen in Room 15, where Gable and Lombard spent their first night of wedded bliss. Lights go on and off with no mortal hand flicking them; footsteps are heard in the room; water taps go on and off; toilets flush when no one is around.

The fact is that these paranormal manifestations happen *all over* the second floor, in *all* of the rooms.

Clark Gable and Carole Lombard

Even the downstairs seems affected; the jukebox sometimes bursts into action with no corporeal assistance.

This must have presented quite a dilemma to the
writers and editors of the supermarket press. But they
found a way out: they simply ignored the rest of the
Oatman Hotel and zeroed in on Room 15.

"I don't think it's Gable and Lombard," Doris Acree,

a chambermaid at the hotel since 1969 told me. "If Gable and Lombard were going to haunt any place, I don't think it would be here. They only spent a couple of nights here in this hotel way back in 1939."

Dolly Miller, at one time one of the owners of the hotel, was quoted in the tabloids as saying, "Sometimes you can hear them [Gable and Lombard] whispering and laughing in there. It's really scary."

Apparently it couldn't have been all that scary, since Miller told me she never said that.

Some *truly* ghostly anecdotes about the hotel, however, have been studiously ignored or avoided by the tabloid press, since they don't fit in with the Gable and Lombard story.

Billie Jo Trammel, present owner of the hotel, told me of some strange occurrences: "The upstairs has now been set aside as a museum. The rooms were left just as they had been rented up until 1975. One time in one of the rooms I noticed that there was dust all over the bedspread, except there was an outline as if a human being had been lying on the bed. A few weeks later I saw the same thing. The rooms are all closed off with screens. You have to have screwdrivers and so on to get in. And there's nothing to indicate that anyone sat on the bed and then lay down; it's as if a body was laid down and lifted up."

Trammel also told of a dog's apparent sighting of something from a different dimension: "There was this poodle that would run to. the Theater Room, where we have the theater artifacts, and would jump around and bark as though he was playing with someone, but there was no one there. It wasn't an angry or warning bark, it was a playful bark."

Only one apparition seems to have been sighted, and that was of a chambermaid. Miller told of a man who checked out and left a dollar tip for a chambermaid who he said had opened his door early that morning to leave clean towels. He gave the tip to one of Miller's co-owners, Judy Whittaker, to pass on to the chambermaid. Whittaker assumed he had seen their only chambermaid, wearing the hotel's trademark, a "sidearm"— a show gun designed to evoke the atmosphere of the Old West. But when that chambermaid turned up at 8 A.M., she said she had not been in the building since the day before. "It must have been the ghost of someone who had worked in the building years and years ago," Miller said.

There are, however, some interesting, and seemingly more legitimate, stories about Gable and Lombard set in the wide world beyond Oatman, Arizona. We might start in Indianapolis.

Lombard was a devotee of Nellie Meier, who lived in Indianapolis and was world famous as a palm reader during the first half of this century. Meier was visited by such famous people as Eleanor Roosevelt, Joan Crawford, Mary Pickford, and both the senior and junior Douglas Fairbanks. She was a close friend of Albert Einstein, and Sergei Rachmaninoff gave a private piano recital in her house. She went to Europe twenty-nine times, and world leaders—Winston Churchill among them—flocked to her.

Lombard often visited Meier, whom she called Aunt Nellie. On the last day of her life, Lombard was in Indianapolis on a war bond tour, and she took time to go to Meier's house for a reading. According to legend, Meier warned Lombard not to take the plane to the

West, but the actress went from Meier's house to the airport—a few hours later, Lombard was dead.

Kenny Kingston is a southern California psychic who knows many film and TV celebrities. (A series of spot checks indicates that they also know him and have favorable things to say about him.) Kingston told me that after Lombard's plane crashed, Gable immediately flew to the site. This puzzled people, since her body was incinerated in the crash. Some time later, Kingston says, Gable told him this story.

When Lombard was about to start on her bond tour, Gable had a premonition of danger and tried to persuade her not to go. She was determined to make the tour, however. Their discussion got a bit heated, to the extent she took off a gold topaz earring he had given her, threw it at him, and stormed out. Gable, in flying to the site of the crash, was looking for the other earring, which he assumed Lombard probably put into her purse rather than wear a single earring. He did not find it.

Since Gable's death, Kingston says that he has been in touch with Gable's spirit as well as that of Lombard's. To quote Kingston, Gable's spirit told him, "Now the earrings are a mate in Paradise."

And if that isn't a romantic ending to this chapter, I don't know what is.

2
JUDY GARLAND AND THE RUNWAY LIGHTBULB

Larry Davies is a pianist and artist with a wide circle of friends in the New York theatrical-artistic world. One of them was Judy Garland. He has many memories of Judy, such as the grocery-store tomato argument, the shaving-cream fight, the purloined milk bottles, and, most important, the indestructible runway light bulb.

He still has that light bulb, and a photo of it appears in this chapter. He acquired the bulb in 1968 at Garland's last performance, in New York. She died in June of 1969.

"After I became friends with Judy, I went to almost all her shows in New York," Davies told me. "I think this was New Year's Eve. I'd been there two or three nights. She saw me standing at the side of the runway. It was her last curtain call and the crowd was going crazy. She came over to me and took my hand in hers and put it on one of the bulbs in the runway, and looking me straight in the eye she said, 'This will always be with you.' It was as though she had said, 'Take this, this is part of me.' So I unscrewed it and put it in my pocket. I've had it for twenty years.''

Davies left New York and moved to Key West, Florida, in 1976. He acquired a showplace house, where he lived until it burned to the ground. "The whole house was gutted,'' Larry says, "except for that light bulb, which was still intact. There seemed to be some sort of energy there. I couldn't understand why it wouldn't break. Chandeliers melted. It was eight hours of intense heat. I didn't get anything out of that house but that light bulb. I was stunned by the fact that it wasn't even smoke-damaged. I think she's very much around and her energy is involved with that bulb. It kind of freaked me out. I get a feeling of security from that little bulb. In fact, anybody who is psychic and visits me is drawn to that little bulb; they have a feeling of its energy. I never tell anybody about it unless they ask.''

Lynn Gardner, a psychic who lives in Indianapolis, was in Key West a few years ago giving lectures and demonstrations of metaphysical occurrences. Larry got to know her and asked her to come to his new house, hold a séance, and try to bring in Judy.

"My perceptions when she came through,'' Gardner told me, "were that Larry was very special to her, that she trusted him and knew that he really cared, that he was in her corner at all times. She mentioned that one time in her silliness she covered him with shaving cream. She just decided to have a little shaving cream fight with him. Just playfulness. I guess they messed up the apartment pretty good with shaving cream. It was that kind of energy that she had, a very playful, loving energy. She was there to remind Larry of the good times they had had."

Gardner says she had no idea beforehand of this shaving-cream caper; it was a private, unimportant thing that Davies had probably never mentioned to anyone, at least not to Gardner.

"She also," Gardner continued, "showed us the time their car had broken down late at night in New York. So they hopped a ride with a milk truck, and she managed to help herself to a couple of bottles of milk. She hid them in the pockets of her fur coat. I didn't know anything about that either, but Larry said it happened. Those were the kinds of things that came through as points of reference for him. He was still worried about Judy, and her main message was, 'I'm okay.'

"She tried to sing through me. It was like she was trying to force my vocal cords. But I stopped; I was not comfortable with that. I could see her and hear her. She seemed very happy and youthful; she did not feel old or tragic at all. She was not morbid or traumatized at all. The way I experienced her that day was as she was at her peak. She was happy. It was like she was still singing on the other side."

Garland died in London at the age of forty-seven, a magnificent public performer with a tragic private life. When she was a child the studios kept her on a regimen of stimulants and depressants that, along with the other pressures of a film star's existence, put her under psychiatric care while she was still in her teens. In her obituary in the *New York Times* she was quoted: "They'd give us pep pills. Then they'd take us to the studio hospital and knock us cold with sleeping pills.

Judy Garland as she appeared in The Wizard of Oz *in 1939*

After four hours they'd wake us up and give us pep pills again. That's the way we worked, and that's the way we got thin. That's the way we got mixed up. And that's the way we lost contact."

The runway lightbulb

(Photo courtesy of Larry Davies)

She married five times. She had great successes professionally—and dismal failures, too. Toward the end of her life, the failures were predominant.

Davies met Judy in 1966, and they became close friends. "At the time," he says, "She was like a little roaming gypsy, going from pillar to post. It was a very vulnerable time for her. Whenever she would find someone who would listen without any 'I wants,' trying to get something out of her . . . well, I think that's the reason our relationship clicked so well. She would call at night sometimes and we would talk two or three hours. It was very heavy talk. She would talk about what life was all about. She was a very spiritual woman. She was very hyper at this time. She had no money. She had a couple of good friends in New York who would slip her two or three hundred dollars every now and then. She would go to a little club up around

76th Street and First Avenue. Every night around two or three o'clock she would have to stop at this club. She would sing two or three songs. After she died I was in there, and I found out that the owner would slip her two or three hundred dollars, and she needed that money.

"I remember one time we went shopping in a supermarket; it was a Gristedes, I think. She was all disguised, and she was in the vegetable department. She had picked up some vegetables and put them down and somebody came along and picked them up. They commenced to have an argument. They were snatching tomatoes back and forth. I was in another aisle and heard this commotion. I ran over and got her out of there. When we left I heard the lady, who by this time had realized who Judy was, saying, all excited, to the manager, 'I just had a vegetable fight with Judy Garland!'

"She got to be very down and out. The last time I saw her was in March of 1969. Then she moved to London with her last husband. She was so vulnerable in those days. She'd talk about how people didn't understand her. March was the last time I saw her, and then she called two times from London, and she'd talk two or three hours. She'd call at two or three in the morning, New York time.

"The last time I saw her she said, 'Have you still got that light bulb?' Obviously it was something important to her. At the time I wondered, what's with this cockamamie light bulb, what's the big deal about that?

"I said, 'Yes, ma'am.'"

3
WAS THAT JOHN HODIAK LOOKING IN THE WINDOW?

Hal Gefsky is an actors' agent, vice president of the Agency for Performing Arts, one of the established talent agencies in Hollywood. He considers himself hard-nosed and down-to-earth, but some strange things have happened since he moved into the Beverly Hills house where he now lives.

The house, built before World War II, has an interesting history. The late actor John Hodiak (1914–1955) lived there after marrying actress Anne Baxter. Baxter was a granddaughter of the celebrated architect Frank Lloyd Wright, and Wright added many touches to the house after his granddaughter and her new husband bought it.

Soon after Gefsky moved in, in the mid-1970s, a very intriguing thing happened. Actors often come to Gefsky's home; on this day Simon Oakland, a character actor well known in Hollywood and Broadway, had

John Hodiak

Hal Gefsky's home

been invited with his wife, Lois. Lois is what the old fan magazines would have called "a nonprofessional," which means she is not an actress, director, writer, or anything else to do with The Industry.

"I have a pool table in a room next to the kitchen," Gefsky told me, "and she was in the pool room. She looked out the window and saw a man walking back and forth. He was wearing a hat. We were expecting some more people, and she assumed he was one of them. So she called me and said, 'There's a man out back and he's obviously come around to the side door instead of coming to the front door.' I asked her where she'd seen him, and she said out the window. Well, that room she was in was on the second floor. The house is on a hill. So I walked her around outside and showed her. To see somebody outside the window he'd have to be about fifteen feet tall."

Lois, however, insisted she had seen this man walking back and forth just outside the window. "She said she saw this guy very plainly," Gefsky says, "and she's a very solid woman. She was a head nurse at Queens Hospital in New York. I asked her if she knew him, and she said no. I didn't know what to make of it.

"A short time later the Oaklands moved to Palm Springs. One night she was watching an old movie and all of a sudden she called out to her husband. 'Si,' she said, 'that's the man I saw at Hal Gefsky's place that night. He's that actor there!'

"It was John Hodiak. She had never seen him before."

One sometimes hears stories about ghosts who walk above the floor, or six inches below it. In some cases, it turns out that the floor had been at the higher or lower level when the ghosts were presumably living. I asked Gefsky if that might have been the case with this house, but he insisted that it could not have been. He had seen photographs of the house from its earliest days, and there had never been any solid support where Lois says she saw the man walking. And since Wright had put his stamp on the house, Gefsky says, nobody would dream of crass alterations.

"It's said that Hodiak had his best years here," Gefsky says. "It was his honeymoon house, so he was happy. I guess he was a happy ghost who came around and enjoyed himself."

More recently, Gefsky entertained in his home psychic Kenny Kingston and some other guests. They spoke of the apparition, and then the conversation turned to other matters. At one point, a woman left the group to make a call to her daughter. She returned soon after and said nervously, "There was a man's voice on the line while I was making my call. He just kept saying 'Hello' in a faint voice. I finally hung up because I thought someone else was trying to use the phone." Gefsky told her that she had been the only one using the phone at the time.

Kingston says he immediately thought, "Ah, Mr. Hodiak is back again, drawn here by the fact that we were talking about him."

A little later in the evening, Gefsky got a phone call that confused him. The caller, who was from his alarm service, told him someone had pushed their button. "It's a push-button sort of alarm," Gefsky says. "You push it and they call you right back. It's for help when somebody's sick or that kind of thing. Or it could be a burglar alarm. But nobody had been near the button. That's the only time that anything of that kind has ever happened."

Kingston has his own interpretation of this event, and that is that Gefsky's burglar alarm was very sensitive—sensitive enough to record the visit of a spirit.

4
IDA LUPINO GETS A GHOSTLY PHONE CALL

Phone calls from the dead seem outlandish, but while they don't exactly clutter up the phone lines, they are not as uncommon as one might expect. Two writers on parapsychology, D. Scott Rogo and Raymond Bayliss, ran across enough of them to publish a book titled *Phone Calls from the Dead* in 1970. The book recounts seventy-five cases. "They're a lot more common than anyone ever believed," Rogo told me.

One such case, published three decades ago in a book called *Spooks Deluxe,* by the columnist Danton Walker, involved Ida Lupino, a successful Hollywood actress, director, and producer.

Lupino was born into a noted English theatrical family. Her father and mother were prominent in the English variety theater. Andrew Meyer, a fictitious name given by Lupino, was a close friend of the family. Young Ida called him Uncle Andy.

Ida Lupino as a young actress

"At the time," Lupino wrote to Walker, "we were living with my grandmother at her home in the outskirts of London while my parents—whom I always called by their first names, Stanley and Connie—were playing an engagement in a variety house."

One night when she was nine, Lupino related, she

had a disturbing dream about Uncle Andy. She went downstairs to tell her grandmother, who was in the kitchen preparing a late supper for Stanley and Connie, due back from the theater. While Ida was telling her grandmother about the dream, the phone rang. Her grandmother asked the little girl to answer it.

"I went to the phone," Lupino wrote Walker, "took the phone off the hook and heard a voice on the line, but it was so faint I could scarcely understand the words. Finally, the voice became stronger and I could understand the message, repeated monotonously several times: 'I must talk to Stanley. It is terribly important.' "

Lupino recognized the voice as that of Uncle Andy, and said her father wasn't home yet. But the voice, now quite distinct, kept saying the same thing over and over. She called her grandmother to the phone and heard her say, "Why Andy, are you *ill?* I'll ask Stanley to call you the moment he comes in."

Then the call was cut off. Her grandmother protested angrily to the operator, who insisted there had not been a call on the line in the past hour. Lupino's parents returned a half hour later and she told them what had happened. They were visibly upset and tried to send her to bed.

Her grandmother protested. "She's not mistaken, Stanley," she said, "and I think you had better call Andy. He sounded as though he was ill."

Lupino wrote that she has never forgotten how tense her father's voice sounded when he answered.

"Mom," he said, "Andrew Meyer is dead. He hung himself three days ago."

5
AUDREY MEADOWS AND HER NICE GHOST

O ne of the problems of writing a book of this sort is that celebrities are invariably barricaded behind phalanxes of receptionists, secretaries, administrative assistants, managers, agents, and other entourages of various sorts, shapes, and shoe sizes—all of whom consider their role to be preventing anyone short of the chairman of the board of NBC, the president of the United States, Robert Redford, or a really good hairdresser from getting through to their employers.

In preparing this chapter on Audrey Meadows, I thought for one brief, shining moment that I might have the system licked, or at least temporarily subdued. By tortuous degrees, I had reached her manager of thirty-five years, and he seemed quite amenable to helping me interview Miss Meadows. She was getting ready for a trip to the Orient, he said, but wouldn't be

The cast of "The Honeymooners": Jackie Gleason, Audrey Meadows, Art Carney, and Joyce Randolph

leaving for a few days. He'd get in touch with her about my project.

The next day he called back and told me apologetically that Miss Meadows's maid had decided that her mistress was just too busy for this sort of thing. "I guess it's the trip to China," he murmured lamely.

Oh well, you can't win 'em all—and now and then a reporter does manage to slip by the maid. As evidence is an interesting article from the January 1964 issue of *Fate* magazine written by Dick Kleiner, a Scripps-Howard entertainment reporter. In the article, Meadows describes an experience she had when she was twenty-one years old, long before she was making television history as Mrs. Ralph Kramden.

Few who see Meadows to this day—or, more likely, to

this late night—in her role opposite Jackie Gleason in "The Honeymooners" know that she is a trained singer. At twenty-one, she had just landed a part in the chorus of a summer-stock musical company in Montclair, New Jersey. Another woman in the show invited her to room with her at Mrs. N's rooming house, and she accepted. The second-floor room had obviously once been occupied by a child; children's books lined the bookcase and a lampshade was covered with nursery rhymes.

It was a hot, humid summer, and one night, before the roommates went to sleep, they opened the window wide. The next morning it was shut tight. They wondered if it had slipped, but the same thing happened the next night. Meadows asked Mrs. N if she had come in during the night to shut the window, but the landlady said she had not. The girls were skeptical; one night they shoved a heavy dresser in front of the door. The next morning it was still in place, and the window was closed. Sometimes they propped up the window with a ruler, only to find the next morning that the ruler was on the ground outside and the window was down.

Meadows observed something else strange about the room. She noticed one day that a copy of *Black Beauty* had been pulled halfway out on one of the shelves of the bookcase. Bemused, she pushed it back, only to find it pulled out the next morning.

These events continued for several nights. Meadows's roommate said that there had to be some rational explanation. But Meadows, whose mother was psychic and who was psychic herself, felt that something otherworldly was going on. She could feel something strange about the room—in some places more than others. The area of the bookcase gave her a particularly eerie sensation.

One day, over a cup of tea, she asked her landlady if a child had ever lived in the room. Mrs. N was visibly shaken but reluctantly admitted it had been her son's room and that he had died in that room at the age of twelve.

Meadows asked if *Black Beauty* had been his favorite book, and the startled landlady said it had. Meadows then told Mrs. N that she felt the room was being haunted by the dead child.

Mrs. N began to sob, but when she regained her composure she said it made her really happy to hear Meadows's conjectures.

"I've had the strangest feeling lately about my boy," she said, "that he is near me. Only I couldn't believe it. I've never believed in ghosts. But to hear you say it makes me think I was right."

Mrs. N then told Meadows the circumstances of her son's death. One night she had left the window open, and there was a sudden cold snap. The boy took cold and died of pneumonia shortly thereafter.

Meadows felt this could be why the boy's spirit compulsively closed the window at night when he returned to read his favorite book. The manifestations continued through the summer, but Meadows now enjoyed them, feeling that her visitor was just the innocent spirit of a boy who wanted to be near his mother and the scenes of his short earthly life.

Meadows told the reporter that she had had many psychic experiences throughout her life, but that this was one of the most pleasant.

"Ghosts can be very nice people," she said.

6
WHAT MARILYN MONROE WANTS KNOWN

This chapter involves John Myers and Kenny Kingston, two highly intriguing psychics who have demonstrated supernormal powers beyond doubt, and their dealings with Marilyn Monroe.

The late John Myers was a man of unusual attainments on both the mystical and the mundane levels. He began as a dental surgeon in England, became a spiritual healer, a recognized portrait painter, a business executive, and—most important for this account—a man in whose presence paranormal things happened to photographs. "Extras," which is parapsychologese for faces and forms of people not visibly present when the pictures taken, appeared on pictures Myers took or that were taken in his presence. Some of these people were unknown; some were recognizable people who were dead. Some were famous. Marilyn Monroe is one of them.

Marilyn Monroe

Perhaps the definitive account of Myers's life and psychic activities is a book written by Maurice Barbanell, *He Walks in Two Worlds*. Barbanell, who knew Myers well, was the founder and for many years editor of *Psychic News*, a widely circulated British newspaper on psychic matters.

Myers, a successful dentist, became interested in psychic phenomena and soon discovered he had extraordinary qualities, both as a healer and as a psychic photographer. Some famous people whose likenesses appeared on photographs Myers took or on those taken in his presence early in his career include authors Edgar Wallace and Israel Zangwill. An image that closely resembled Benjamin Disraeli, the nineteenth-century British prime minister, also appeared. Much was written about Myers; through this publicity he met an American who changed the course of his life.

In 1935, a wealthy New Yorker named R. Laurence Parish was visiting London on business. Parish was president of a firm called American Flange & Manufacturing Co. As a result of a motorcycle accident when he was in his teens, he had experienced severe sciatica throughout his life. He had seen many specialists in the United States and in Europe to no avail, and had resigned himself to a life of constant pain. In addition to his physical suffering, his already failing vision worsened with each year. When he arrived in London, the lenses he was wearing were near the maximum strength that could be prescribed. Parish sought out Myers not for healing, however, but out of curiosity about psychic photography, of which he had been unaware before reading an article about Myers.

The two took an immediate liking to each other. Myers gave Parish a demonstration of psychic photography, and extras appeared on two of the photographic plates. Parish was highly impressed, but decided to buy his own camera and developing and printing materials. Another séance was arranged in Parish's hotel suite, this time using Parish's equipment. Again there were supernormal results.

Still not completely convinced, Parish bought another expensive camera, this time a Reflex press camera with a large telescopic lens, and hired two professional photographers to take the pictures. Again a series of extras was obtained. These included some well-known British figures who had died, as well as written messages involving Parish's family.

Convinced of Myers's authenticity, Parish asked if Myers's other powers—his healing powers—would have a salutary effect on his sciatica. According to Barbanell's account, Myers healed Parish overnight. The following day, he had no pain, he no longer limped, he no longer had to wear heavy clothing because of the discomfort cold had produced. Thirty years later, Parish was still alive and feeling well; his sciatica never returned. In addition, Myers healed the industrialist's faulty eyesight. Within a week, he was able to read without glasses for the first time since his childhood; that cure too was permanent.

Apparently, Parish did not intend to let his amazing new friend get away from him. He suggested that Myers would find expanded opportunities for his psychic talents in the New World and urged him to come to New York as his assistant. Myers assented, and eventually became the general manager and vice president of Parish's company. He continued his demonstrations of psychic photography in this country and appeared on the TV programs of such hard-nosed skeptics as Jack Paar and Mike Wallace. Wallace pulls no punches, and often gives interviewees short shrift. He prepared for Myers by buying a packet of photographic paper at a shop undisclosed to Myers. After Myers's demonstration, when the pictures were developed in the television studio, extras appeared on them, although Myers never touched them. Some of the extras were shown to the television audience.

Myers's reputation as an artist was also burgeoning. His portrait of the former Indian prime minister Pandit Nehru hangs in the Indian Parliament Building. He painted portraits of Cardinal Spellman and George Gershwin. But perhaps his most intriguing sitter was Marilyn Monroe.

They came to know each other well. She lived close to his apartment in New York, and they had neighboring houses in Connecticut. He gave her healing and also painted her portrait, which was awarded a prize at a UNICEF exhibition at the United Nations.

At their first meeting, Barbanell wrote, Myers found Marilyn a nervous wreck. "You could look in her eyes and tell," Myers said. "The way she spoke was strange. She seemed far away."

Myers urged her not to take sleeping pills or drugs. Her third marriage, to playwright Arthur Miller, had just ended, and she was in the grip of a deep melancholy. She had changed her religion and adopted Miller's Jewish faith; now she was unable to make up her mind what faith she wanted to follow. This was causing acute frustration and emotional upset. Religion became one of the main subjects of conversation between Myers and Marilyn while he was painting her, particularly since he was also Jewish.

"She was lonely and had no really close friends," Myers recalled. "I never thought of her as a great film star. To me she was the modern Mona Lisa, an American Mona Lisa, a lovely girl with an extraordinarily sweet, sad, enigmatic smile."

Kenny Kingston

After her death, according to Barbanell, Myers said that Marilyn appeared to him several times, and that she emphasized that she had died as a result of an accidental overdose of barbiturates, not suicide. She had been unable to sleep, was desperately alone, and had taken pill after pill.

"I did not understand that I was poisoning myself," Myers said her earthbound spirit told him. "It was then too late."

Marilyn died in 1962 at the age of thirty-six. Three years later, Myers was in California on business with two salesmen for his company, Dan Spencer and Jud Longaker, at the Beverly Hills Hotel. They decided to visit Marilyn's crypt and take some photographs. Extras appeared, including likenesses of Marilyn.

In the late 1970s, Walter Uphoff, a well regarded parapsychologist who lives in Wisconsin, was visiting the London offices of *Psychic News*. He copied statements that the two company employees had written to Myers, and he has generously provided them for this book. The statements are similar. Here is part of Spencer's.

"As you will recall, you suggested that you would like to pay your respects to the grave of Marilyn Monroe. . . . I bought two film cartridges for the Kodak Instamatic camera from the drug store in the hotel. I loaded the camera and took several pictures of you standing beside Marilyn's crypt, and I took several pictures of Mr. Longaker standing there, also. Then you and Mr. Longaker took several pictures of me and the crypt where Marilyn's body is entombed.

"We mailed the films to the processor and I have just received the prints back from you. I am amazed at the extras which appear on these color photographs. They are completely mysterious as far as I am concerned. There was nothing visible which could have caused the images to appear when we took those pictures. I am very interested in the results; however, I cannot explain them."

Kenny Kingston calls himself psychic to the stars. A flamboyant type, he at first blush seems like a television evangelist on a New Age kick. Nevertheless, his abilities compel respect. He not only says he knows famous entertainers and other people in high places on the Hollywood scene, but they seem to know *him*. He says he's been on "The Merv Griffin Show" more than fifty times, which may or may not be a recommendation, but at least it indicates he's impressing somebody.

One Los Angeles TV executive, Peter Schlesinger, was very high on Kingston. He told me, "Kingston is very good at what he does. I've seen him perform at nightclubs and at seminars. He reads people. He takes somebody's watch or ring and tells them about themselves."

Does he communicate with spirits, too?

Schlesinger said, "I can't verify that he's talking with spirits. I've never seen him do that, but that doesn't mean he doesn't do it."

The first time I talked with Kingston on the phone, I was slightly put off by his voluble name dropping, his gee-whiz fan magazine approach to film stars. But about fifteen minutes into the conversation he gave me a spontaneous demonstration of his psychic powers. "You're sitting in a big house," he told me. I was, but that could have been a lucky guess. I asked him about something that was then going on in my career, and he gave me an answer that was disappointing but turned out later to be quite true, including what the specific problem was. During another conversation, he told me I was having a slight difficulty with one of my eyes, which was true, and he impressed me with his apparent mediumistic abilities.

In spite of his Hollywood persona, Kenny Kingston impressed me.

In 1954, Kingston was living in San Francisco. He was a close friend of the late actor Clifton Webb. (In fact, he says he still is.)

"Clifton called me from Beverly Hills," Kingston told me, "and said there was a Mrs. DiMaggio who wanted to see me. She had just married Joe DiMaggio, and I didn't make the connection. Clifton made the appointment for her for nine in the evening. About 9:15 she hadn't arrived. I flipped off the outside lights and started to go down the hallway, and the doorbell rang. I opened the door and there she stood. Of course, instantly I recognized her.

"She was breathless. She was wearing a black coat with an ermine collar. That's how our relationship began. She came to me on a fairly regular basis in San Francisco, where she lived then, and later when we were both in southern California.

"Most of what we used to talk about is confidential, and also, I give what is called a semi-trance reading, so I really wouldn't remember anyway. But she was rarely depressed. About three days before she passed away, she rang me up. She was jubilant, extremely happy. She said she'd been reinstated by the studio and was going back to work. She was ecstatic about that. She sent me a beautiful neckpiece, a gold chain. Inscribed on it was, 'Love is the one immortal thing about us. Without love, what else can life mean?' I still have that.

"Earlier, she had invited me to see a house she was

going to buy in Brentwood, and I went with her. I thought it was too dreary for her. The trees threw very dramatic shadows. I just thought the place wasn't suitable for Marilyn. But she loved the house and wanted to buy it. That's the house where she passed away.

"After she passed, I had contact with her before a year was up. It was at a séance, a regular séance that we used to hold at Clifton's house. Marilyn came and said that she did not commit suicide. It was an accidental overdose; a little too much alcohol and a few too many barbiturates.

"I've had contact with her a number of times since then. When we had our fifteenth anniversary séance in Malibu for Marilyn in 1977, she said that Elvis Presley would be the next major star to go into paradise, and he passed soon after that.

"Recently I was driving to a parapsychology meeting with a friend of mine, a Dr. Schramm. I was giving a lecture. We turned onto the street where the club was located, and I noticed it was called Capri Street. I said, 'Marilyn always said she would love to go to the isle of Capri.' As we started to get out of the car, Dr. Schramm noticed a long, red fingernail on the floor. I had had the car cleaned the day before and nobody had been in the car since but us. I put the fingernail into an envelope. It was an apport from Marilyn.

"A couple of months later I was doing the Mike Douglas show, and I mentioned the fingernail. I brought the envelope out and handed it to Mike. It popped out of the envelope onto the floor. Mike and I got down on the floor trying to find it, and we finally did, with thousands watching. It was a real fingernail. It was an apport from Marilyn."

7
ELKE SOMMER'S SCARY HOUSE

A little more than twenty years ago, the venerable *Saturday Evening Post* ran an account of a haunted house in Beverly Hills' Benedict Canyon. A year later, it ran another article—on the same house and the same people—with the latest development, a mysterious fire.

The writer of these articles was Joe Hyams, who lived in the house with his wife, beautiful German movie actress Elke Sommer.

Let us examine the situation that prevailed in Benedict Canyon.

It was early July 1964, and Sommer and Hyams had moved into the house only a few days before. Hyams was out, and Elke had invited a German journalist, Edith Dahlfield, for afternoon coffee. As Elke was about to pour, her visitor mentioned seeing a man standing in the hall who had just gone into the dining

Elke Sommer

room. Elke walked into the dining room, but found it was empty, as was the kitchen beyond. Dahlfield insisted she had seen a man and described him as husky, broad-shouldered, around fifty years old and wearing dark slacks, a white shirt, and a black tie. His hair was thinning, she said, and he had a bulbous, "potato" nose.

The next incident happened about two weeks later. Elke's mother, who was staying with them, was sleeping in a downstairs room. She said she woke up to find a man staring at her. She insisted he was standing at the foot of her bed, and that just as she was about to scream for help, he vanished.

"It was about that time that we became aware of another phenomenon," Hyams wrote. "Almost every night after we went to bed we began hearing noises coming from the direction of the dining room. It sounded as though there had been a dinner party and the chairs were being pushed back as the guests rose."

Early in August, Elke and her mother went to Yugoslavia, where Elke was making a film. Hyams planned to stay home and join them in a few weeks. Alone in the house, he constantly found a window open that he had shut and locked; he heard the front door open and close, even though it was bolted. He bought electronic equipment such as portable radios, tape recorders, and radio transmitters. He outlined the positions of the legs of the chairs in the dining room with chalk. The listening equipment picked up the sound of the chairs being moved, although when he checked they still stood squarely in their chalk marks.

Feeling uncomfortable, Hyams invited a friend named Gordon Mueller to stay with him, although he did not say anything about the "ghost." For a few days, all seemed quiet; then it was time for Hyams to join his wife and mother-in-law in Europe. Mueller's apartment was being redecorated, and Hyams told him he could stay in the house.

When Hyams arrived in Yugoslavia, he found a letter from Mueller telling of strange noises and a window that mysteriously came open. Later, Hyams got another letter from Mueller saying the house was "creepy." He wrote: "I have never experienced anything like this before. Every time I go into the dining room the hair on the back of my neck rises up."

While Mueller was in the house, Hyams arranged for a private detective to check the place periodically. He received letters from the detective saying that he constantly found windows and doors wide open, although nothing was missing and Mueller said he always locked the house up tight. One time when Mueller was away, the detective kept the place under close surveillance, and reported that at about 2:30 in the morning all the lights in the house suddenly went on. Before he reached the house, they all went off. An electrician was hired to check the fuse box and lines, and reported that everything was in order. The fuse box had no master switch that would enable a practical joker to turn all the lights on or off at once.

Around Christmas 1964, Hyams and Elke returned home. They continued to hear the noises in the dining room every night, but found they were getting used to them.

Things continued to happen. They were away a good part of the spring of 1965, and asked a friend, Joe Kavanagh, to look in on the house every now and then. Kavanagh later told them that no matter how carefully he locked the place, the next time he came by a door would be open.

That August, Elke and Hyams went to the beach for the summer. When Hyams returned to get mail, the man who cleaned their swimming pool, Marvin Chandler, asked him who was staying in the house.

"No one," Hyams replied.

"That's what I thought," Chandler said, "but last Tuesday afternoon I saw a man in the dining room—a big man about six feet tall, heavy-built, with a white shirt and black tie. When I went to the door to ask him when you were coming back he disappeared—just seemed to evaporate in front of my eyes."

In early September, Hyams wrote, a writer friend named John Sherlock asked if he could stay in the house for a couple of days. He was a young Englishman possessed, Hyams said, of an analytical mind and a cool temperament, and Hyams felt he would be the ideal no-nonsense observer. So Hyams was surprised when the next morning Sherlock phoned to say he was at a hotel.

Hyams wrote, "From the moment he entered the house alone at about 11 P.M., he told me, he had a strong feeling that someone was watching him. 'I went to bed in the downstairs guest room at about 12:45,' he said. 'I felt a light on in the hallway. I felt certain someone was near and turned around. In the doorway I saw the figure of a man almost six feet tall staring at me. He was wearing dark trousers, a white shirt, and a dark tie. I have never had such a feeling of menace.

" 'I got out of bed, got dressed and looked into the hallway to see if he was still there. He wasn't, but as I went down the hallway I could feel him. I couldn't leave the house fast enough.' "

Hyams clung to a there-must-be-a-rational-explanation-for-all-this point of view. In his 1966 *Saturday Evening Post* article, he wrote, "Neither of us had seen the ghost personally and I believe only what I can see."

Twenty years later, he expressed what struck me as a healthy confusion.

"You get involved with so many kooks in your life," he told me, "and I've had enough without getting involved with people who believe in ghosts."

"You don't believe in ghosts?" I asked.

"I'd never buy a house again if someone told me it was haunted," he replied. "I believe there are things I don't know anything about, and I really don't want to know anything about them either, so I'll stay away from them—and that goes for ghosts. I don't really believe in what I can't see, but I do know there are things I can't see that exist. Isn't that a roundabout answer?"

There seems to have been a lot of evidence for something paranormal going on in your house, I ventured.

"Elke never saw the ghost, nor did I," Hyams replied. "We were surrounded by people who *claimed* they saw a ghost and who reported basically the same presence in terms of physical description, clothing, and so forth. We were aware there was something in the house that made us uncomfortable, yes."

Back then, Hyams was thrashing about desperately for a twentieth-century, meat-and-potatoes explanation for these happenings. He had dinner one night with a writer who sounds as though he had been on too many movie sets. The writer suggested that the house contained hidden rooms and passageways, that there was an unknown roomer, a mortal freeloader. Hyams had an architect check the blueprints and the house itself. Nothing.

Hyams went so far as to hire a team of termite inspectors to check under the house to see if any of the little beasts might have chewed a hole in the bottom of the house through which a heavy man with a white shirt and black pants—or anybody else—could have made an entrance. The place was innocent of termites, or of any exotic entryways.

Someone told Elke and Hyams that ghosts prefer to stay in familiar places, so they decided to make some changes in the dining room, where the ghost had been seen frequently. They changed the light fixtures, repainted the room, and papered one wall near where the apparition had been most often reported.

In light of subsequent developements, this might have been a dramatically poor idea. It's not nice to fool with Mother Nature.

No top-notch ghost drama—as this certainly is— would be complete without a canine actor or two. And sure enough, the two dogs of the house began acting strangely. They barked while staring into the dining room. The puppy would frequently run to a particular spot in the room, then walk out as though following at someone's heels.

By this time, Hyams was willing to grant that *something* was going on; the next question was *what*. He knew a psychiatrist at the University of California Neuropsychiatric Institute, who passed him on to a resident in psychiatry at the U of C Medical School. She was Dr. Thelma Moss, a well-known parapsychologist with wide experience in the investigation of hauntings. In collaboration with the American Society for Physical Research (ASPR) and Dr. Gertrude R. Schmeidler, a notable New York parapsychologist, a full-scale investigation was launched, and a paper for the society's *Journal* was duly produced, complete with abstract, method, introduction, procedure, scoring, results, statistics, graphs, discussions, references, and all the baggage dear to the hearts of psychologists, straight and para-. To make a long dissertation short, there seemed to be agreement that that house sure was haunted.

Various psychics were brought to the place. No publicity was available about the house at this time; the psychics were given no information as to who the owners were or what anyone had experienced there. As in any well-conducted investigation of this sort, the psychics were "blind." Elke and Hyams were asked to be away from the house, if possible, when the investigators were brought in. If they did meet one of the psychics, they were urged not to give their names or professions. Demonstrations of mind reading were not what was being sought.

Several of the psychics saw clairvoyantly the same apparition that other people had earlier seen visually. One, Douglas Johnson, went directly to the dining room and announced that he saw clairvoyantly a man who once had a moustache and who was very fond of music. "He is a heavy-set man, a European, who spent his past life giving of himself," Johnson said.

Another psychic, Lotte von Strahl, saw a person similiar in appearance, but had a quite different assessment of his personality. Immediately upon entering the house she went to the dining room. Von Strahl described a "monster," a man who was large, untidy, full of hate, and also quite drunk. She shuddered and emitted a low scream. "He touched me!" she exclaimed. "He hates me. He wants me to get out, and I'm afraid of him."

Maxine Bell, who has done successful work with the Los Angeles Police Department in locating lost objects and missing persons, toured the house quickly, then returned to the dining room where she said she saw a sloppy man in his fifties. "I think he is a doctor," she said. "He died of a heart attack at the age of fifty-eight before he could finish something important with the man of the house."

Psychic Brenda Crenshaw went directly to the dining room and said, "I see a man above average height, about fifty-eight years of age, a doctor who died of a chest or heart condition outside the country."

When I spoke to Brenda recently, she said, "I don't remember a great deal about it at all, it was a long time ago. But I certainly saw the man in the corner of a room, wearing a white shirt."

One psychic, Michael Hughes, had a different report. He walked past the dining room and went out near the swimming pool. He said, "I see a blond girl about seventeen years old who died in Europe about three years ago of something in the lungs. She was ill six weeks before passing over. . . The girl is volunteering information that since her death the house she lived in in Europe was burned."

In his *Saturday Evening Post* article, Hyams wrote: "These reports were rather startling. The physical description of the male ghost seemed to fit a doctor with whom I had been writing a book. He had died suddenly before we had finished. It also resembled Elke's father in some respects. The young girl whom Mr. Hughes saw made Elke jump with fright. The description precisely fitted a girl she once knew whose house had burned since her death."

The ASPR suggested that séances be held to try to make contact with the spirits, and five were held. Hyams puts it this way: "Though they were long on showmanship, with much panting and wheezing on the part of the mediums, they were not very long on information."

Von Strahl attempted an exorcism and pronounced, "He's leaving." Subsequent events indicate she may have been overly optimistic.

A clairvoyant named Jacqueline Eastlund visited the house and said she saw a man between forty and sixty, and that he had been murdered by strangulation in the house. She was frightened and refused to stay in the house. A few months later, she and Hyams had a phone conversation during which she made a remarkable prediction. Hyams taped the conversation, and James Crenshaw used it in his article for *Fate* magazine. Parts of it are as follows:

EASTLUND: I see this house in flames six months from now.

HYAMS: Elke wants to know what the fire has to do with ghosts.

EASTLUND: This is what I was being told. What I got was six months from last night, that it would be better if you went and spent the night in a motel.

HYAMS: Six months from last night. Now let's see, today is the 21st (of March, 1966).

EASTLUND: I don't feel that you are going to own the house two years from now.

At another point, Eastlund told Hyams that neither he nor Elke would be hurt in the fire.

Eastlund was a little off on her timing, but otherwise her prediction was extraordinarily accurate. Hyams began his second *Saturday Evening Post* article:

"Just after sunrise on the morning of March 13 [1967], my wife shook me awake. She whispered that she had heard some noises downstairs, and then someone pounding on our bedroom door. I picked up the .38-caliber revolver, which has lain on our night table for the three years we have lived in our 'haunted' house and got out of bed. Downstairs, I heard muffled laughter. Gun in hand, I unlocked our bedroom and ran into a cloud of thick, black smoke."

Firemen were called and quickly extingushed the fire, which was in only the dining room. Damages were estimated at twenty-five thousand dollars. Elke and Hyams left the house that day and never went back there to live.

There was something quite strange about the fire. Hyams wrote in his second article: "The 'ghost' that had troubled us had been reported most often in our dining-room-and-bar area. Someone had told us that ghosts preferred familiar places, so, in what may have been a foolish effort to chase him, we had redecorated the area completely. This was a section of the house that had been gutted by the fire, a fire hot enough to melt our pewter plates and even our silverware. The experts who later surveyed the fire said it had started on the dining-room table. New wallpaper had been burned off the wall. Only the framework of the new bar remained. A few pieces of glass and wire were all that was left of a new chandelier.

"Although our entire house had wall-to-wall carpeting and floor-to-ceiling drapes, all highly inflammable, the fire had not spread to other rooms. The night before, I had shut the dining-room doors, which might explain why the fire was contained—except that the flames had burned through the doors and into an adjoining hallway."

Several of the mediums who had been to the house pointed to the fire's mysterious beginning, its extreme heat, its sudden end, and the fact that it affected only the dining room. They said there was evidence that it was a "spirit fire"—that is, one set by a ghost.

Hyams mentioned in his second article that he and Elke had been looking for another house. The night before the fire, they had been watching an old movie on TV, the literate and very frightening film *The Haunting*. Hyams says that as he turned out the light he said jokingly, "I wonder what the ghost thinks about our moving. If he has any opinion he'd better express it pretty soon."

Within a few hours, the house was on fire.

Strange things can happen to film and cameras that are presumably around spirits. A photographer hired by the insurance company told Hyams that when he took pictures of the fire damage.

"In one picture of the dining room, part of the wallpaper is blurred in one corner as if it had moved, but the rest of the wall is sharp and clear. There couldn't have been any camera movement. Whatever movement there was was on the wall. And in another picture, of the coffee table in the living room, everything surrounding the table is in focus, but the table itself appears to have moved. I've been photographing fire damage for thirty years, it's my profession. My pictures are always sharp. But not the pictures I took of your house. It's the first time that anything like this has happened to me."

On the other hand, von Strahl had a different idea.

Hyams met her at the burned-out house with a Los Angeles arson investigator who was willing to try anything. Von Strahl sifted through the debris for a reading, and then described in detail a person with whom Hyams had recently had a quarrel. The description also fit a suspected arsonist the police had been seeking. And there was some evidence that a back door may have been forced open. Von Strahl, who had said from the first that there was more than one spirit in the house, assured Hyams that the fire had forced them out.

Hyams was not convinced.

He had tried to rent the house after the first *Saturday Evening Post* article appeared, because he and Elke were going to Europe for a time. Twice, people whom he says had no knowledge of the house's reputation were sent by real estate agents and then refused to enter the place. One of these people was Mrs. Red Buttons, who said the place had an evil aura.

Finally Harry Kanter, a neckwear manufacturer from New York, became interested. Hyams told him the house was supposed to be haunted. Kanter said that was all right, he would be away during the day and it would give his wife somebody to talk to. On that light note, a short-term lease was signed. When they were leaving the house, three months later, the Kanters decided to give a good-bye ghost party. The guests wore sheets, pillow cases, and ghostly makeup. Suddenly, at about 11:30, every light in the house went out, and a terrific crash came from the dining room. A heavy, wrought-iron candelabra had crashed to the floor.

Hyams and Elke finally sold the house to an actress named Diahn Williams. In 1969, she was interviewed on Los Angeles TV station KCOP. She was asked when she first was aware of evidence that the place might really be haunted. She replied: the first night.

"The first night I arrived," she said, "having bought the house and then had it repainted while I was in New York, there were all the lights out except one that wouldn't go out, and none of the others would go on. In the next week or two, the light in the dining room would go out just on its own. I would speak to the light finally, because I began to believe more and more that there was something, and it would go back on again.

"Fortunately for me, the ghost has stayed downstairs, at least to my knowledge. He primarily goes around in the kitchen and the rooms near the kitchen. He makes kitchen cabinets open and close, and sometimes with such ferocity it's incredible. I mean, he would open a cabinet door and slam it shut. He does this usually when I'm in the kitchen.

"Then he plays around with the refrigerator, which makes a lot of racket. The other day I had some friends here who did not believe in the ghost. We were talking about the refrigerator, and at that point it began to make noise. They said, 'You've rigged this refrigerator to make noise.' The next day the refrigerator just stopped cold. When he isn't believed he does terrible tricks.

"I've heard footsteps, too, sometimes when other people have been here. Specifically, he lives in the dining room. I understand that chairs used to move in that room. I haven't seen them move, fortunately."

For the past dozen years, the house has been owned by Dennis and Jayne Eisenberg. "We've never encountered anything about this house being haunted," Jayne told me.

Dennis, a real estate developer, seconded the motion.

One housekeeper was scared off, he admits, but by a television station, not an actual ghost. The station called about doing a program, and she answered the phone. The Eisenbergs were out of town and when they returned she met them at the entry hall with her bags packed.

"Another housekeeper thought she saw something or other," Dennis said, but he didn't put much stock in that.

"During the time I've lived here," he said, "I've heard all kinds of strange noises and all kinds of weird stuff and I've been able to explain it away by the breeze moving the bougainvillea against the house, animals in the attic, stuff like that. I'm of the opinion that the fire in the house was started by rats chewing on the wiring."

What a spoilsport!

I never interviewed Elke. She was in Atlantic City in a play at the time I called Joe. He said he would give me her number if I had anything specific to ask her, but I don't. I mentioned that somebody told me she had recently talked about the haunting on the Joan Rivers TV show.

"I guess someone asked about it," Joe said, "but she was not happy with talking about it," says Hyams. "It's not a subject close to her heart. First of all, for a couple of years every time she'd do an interview they'd ask about it. She's just bored with talking about it."

8
CLIFTON WEBB JUST DOESN'T LIKE WOMEN SITTING IN HIS CHAIR

A lot of ghost stories have been told about the actor Clifton Webb, who hit it big as the resourceful and outrageous Mr. Belvedere in popular mid-century movies.

Webb was a devotee of the occult. He lived in a house that had once been owned by the singer Grace Moore and was convinced she was still around. He was a close friend of Hollywood psychic Kenny Kingston. Kingston held regular séances at Webb's house. Since the actor's death, Kingston claims Webb has become one of his spiritual guides, and they maintain constant contact.

By accident, I came across a story that has not appeared in the rather extensive Webbian ghost literature. Being advised to contact a man named Richard Senate, whom I was told had quite a knowledge of Hollywood ghosts, I did so and he proved most friendly and talka-

Clifton Webb and Dorothy McGuire in The Remarkable Mr. Pennypacker

tive. There was, however, a slight problem: he too was writing a book about ghosts. As they used to say in New York, does Macy's tell Gimbel's? But, as we talked, Senate came up with a personal experience that he gave me permission to use in this book.

Senate works in television, and once shot a segment at Kingston's house. Senate described the event to me:

"Kenny's got this throne that Clifton Webb gave him. He's got it on a shrine, sort of, this chair. Supposedly during séances it moves and rattles and does other weird things.

"We were taping, and we took a break. I went into the living room and there was this chair on a big dais, so I just had to sit in it. And I have to admit that I really, really felt weird sitting in the damn thing. But the interesting thing was that after I got out of it my wife, Debbie, who is psychic, said, 'Oh, I have to try this!'

"Now Kenny doesn't allow people to sit on this chair. But he wasn't there, so she plopped down on it. And she felt something slap her. She jumped out of that chair like it had an electric charge. And something ripped her dress.

"At that point Kenny came out from the back and said, 'You were sitting in Clifton's chair, weren't you?'

"She admitted it, and he said to her with a sly wink, 'Clifton doesn't like women sitting in his chair.'

"Clifton Webb," Senate said, "never hid the fact that he was gay."

9
IN HER NEXT INCARNATION, MAE WEST PLANS TO GET IT RIGHT

Mae West's stage and screen persona was very like her off-camera personality. Her swaying walk and throaty voice underscored what has occurred to many people: sex is really kind of funny. Her on-camera character apparently became an integral part of her. Margaret Hamilton, who made her screen debut as a shocked spinster in My Little Chickadee, starring W. C. Fields and West and is best known as the Wicked Witch of the West in *The Wizard of Oz,* once told me, with some amusement, that West retained her sexy saunter and husky voice after the cameras had stopped rolling. "I think it had become a part of her personality," she said.

West was without doubt one of the earthiest of women, but she was also very much involved in spirituality.

West dealt with many psychics and became something of a psychic herself. Danton Walker, in his book

Mae West

Spooks Deluxe, quotes her description of what she did upon deciding to delve into spiritualism. Upon meeting a well-known practitioner in Los Angeles, West offered her an unlimited amount of money for instructing West on how to develop her own powers. The spiritualist replied that money couldn't buy such knowledge; it had to be attained only by meditation and serious study.

Said West, "She taught me first how to go 'into the silence,' how to blank my consciousness and let the inner voice come through. I then became aware that to some extent I had been doing this all my life. I remember once sitting at a prizefight and having the entire plot of a play come to me, out of nowhere.

"It is that 'inner voice' that tells us what to do at times when outside aid or advice can be of little or no help. The discovery has given me tremendous confidence and a wonderful sense of peace."

West was already a famous movie star when she first investigated learning something about the hereafter without the inconvenience of actually going there. According to Walker, rather than cause an uproar by showing up in person at a spiritualistic conclave held in Los Angeles, West sent her manager, Jim Timoney. Timoney also handled prize-fighters and took along one of his protégés, a young, rough-cut pug named Mickey. They attended a demonstration by Jack Kelly, a psychic from Buffalo, New York. Kelly looked at Mickey, who was sitting in the second row, and rattled off a long Polish name. Mickey turned to Timoney and whispered, "That's my family name," which surprised Timoney because he thought Mickey was of Irish descent. Kelly then told Mickey that his father, thought to have died in an accidental drowning, was in fact murdered. Some time later Mickey found out that this was true. He was so impressed that he eventually developed into a medium himself, receiving messages by "spirit writing" in languages he did not understand. When the messages were in English he often had to go to the dictionary to learn the meaning of some of the words.

West became a devotee of Jack Kelly, often phoning him in Buffalo and inviting him to her home for seances. She gave him many presents, including a five-carat diamond ring and an expensive automobile. They were friends until his death in 1963, and, if one is to credit an article in *Fate* magazine, well after that.

The *Fate* article was written by Brenda Shaw, billed as a longtime friend of West. According to the article, West had turned on the television in her living room one evening and sat down at one end of a couch. Suddenly, before the television came on, she heard the sound of a voice, as though someone were trying to speak but couldn't get the words out.

West is quoted in the *Fate* article as follows:

"First I heard this voice, a deep voice, and I knew it wasn't the television. I couldn't make out what it said but I turned and saw feet—two feet, a man's feet. As I turned I looked at the floor and saw a man's shoes and his legs, or rather, his trousers.

"Then I looked up and there was Jack Kelly sitting on the couch next to me, just as real and solid as he had ever been, only looking much younger than when he died 10 or 12 years ago. There wasn't a line on his face, and he was more than 60 when he passed on."

West said she wasn't frightened, but she *was* shocked, and called for her secretary-bodyguard, who was in the next room. The apparition disappeared before her assistant came. It seemed, West said, to dissolve down through the couch. She said the apparition was clad in a full-dress suit, complete with white tie and tails. A tuxedo was the fanciest clothing she'd ever seen Kelly wear in life.

West said this was the first time she had ever seen an apparition of a person she had known. However, she said, she had once seen a group of "entities" come through the wall of her bedroom. They were, she said, wearing unusual costumes: large hats with plumes and clothes from another era. They seemed to be trying to communicate, but she couldn't hear any words. When she asked them to leave, they did and never came back.

Judging from Walker's book, West seemed to think that the inspiration she received when she went into meditation came from an unconscious "inner voice." However, Kenny Kingston thinks differently. Kingston knew West from the time of his youth, when she often called him for psychic readings. According to his book, *Kenny Kingston's Guide to Health and Happiness*, West was very clairvoyant and had spirit guides who helped her with her writing. She called them "The Forces."

"Sometimes," Kingston wrote, "when she was upset that no one had been able to come up with a script idea, she walked around her room saying, 'Forces, Forces, come to me and help me write a script.' She would begin to hear voices and see images, as the plot was revealed to her. She would summon stenographers to work with her around the clock, as she would lie in bed in a trance-like state, dictating as the spirits entered. Within a short period of time the script was complete."

Who were these generous sharers of their inspiration, I asked Kenny, wondering if one could get in line.

"I think in later years it was Jack Kelly," Kenny told me.

But was he a writer? Could he write screenplays?

"Well," Kenny said, "when you go to the other side you can study things. Mae has had contact with me on many, many instances. She's studying directing, so that when she comes back she can be her own director. She says, 'They've never directed me right before. Next time I'll do it myself and get it right.' "

II
ENTERTAINMENT

10
DICK CLARK'S PSYCHIC EXPERIENCE

I did a certain amount of the preliminary research on this book while standing in line at the supermarket. That is where I habitually look over the *National Enquirer,* the *Examiner,* the *Star,* and other representatives of what some might consider the soft underbelly of journalism.

It's funny, though, how, with all their inaccuracies, blatant invention, and gee-whizism, these sheets are in a way more in tune with the new, deeper consciousness than their more respectable cousins on the newstands. Obviously, you must take what you read in the grocery press with a generous portion of salt, but sometimes they surprise you by being reasonably accurate. One *National Enquirer* story I noticed was headlined: DICK CLARK'S INCREDIBLE PSYCHIC EXPERIENCE.

Dick Clark has been running "American Bandstand," a very successful TV show, for more than thirty years. He also produces many other shows as well as movies. He is a very successful man in show biz.

I clipped the story and put it aside for possible investigation. It languished in my files until one day I was being interviewed on station WPTF in Raleigh, North Carolina, by talk show host Allan Handleman. He mentioned parenthetically that he had read in the *Enquirer* that Dick Clark had had a psychic experience. "I have that story," I said. "I've been meaning to check it out if I can get to Clark."

"Oh, it's true," Handleman said. He told me he had had a long interview with Clark, mainly about music, but at one point had casually mentioned the story. Clark was not too eager to talk about it but said it was indeed true. The story Handleman remembers Clark telling him varies slightly from the *Enquirer*'s but is basically the same.

According to the *Enquirer*, this story happened when "American Bandstand" was based at a Philadelphia TV station. The *Enquirer* quotes Clark as follows:

"I was walking down the hall at the TV station when I ran into an older man who worked there. He'd been ill, so I asked him, 'How are you feeling?' He replied, 'I've had better days, but I'm all right now.'

"A few days later I saw the man's son at a party and commented, 'I saw your dad at the station on Tuesday and he looked a lot better.'

"He looked at me long and hard and asked, 'Do you remember what time it was on Tuesday?' I replied it was around 11 A.M.

"The son said, 'Could you be mistaken? Could it have been someone else?'

"But I shook my head. 'No way,' I said. 'What's the problem?'

"He told me that on Tuesday morning his father had been a patient in the hospital—and just after 11 A.M. his heart had stopped beating for six or seven minutes!

"I couldn't believe what I was hearing. I didn't believe in things of this nature before. It's a mystery I can't explain—how I had seen and talked to a man whose heart had stopped beating at that exact moment in a hospital several miles away.".

This story has a slight hole in it, as we used to say in the newspaper business. It's not clear whether the man had died or just had a near-death experience. Perhaps it's the phraseology; the reporter probably meant the man had died, permanently.

In any case, the story Handleman remembers is slightly different. He said Clark told him that the man had had an office opposite his own. The man had been out sick; this particular morning Clark came in and, through the large window of the man's office, saw him sitting at his desk.

"The man was quiet, reflective, thoughtful," Handleman says. "Clark waved to him and the man waved back."

Clark went into his own office and later that morning heard that the man had died on the operating table a short time before.

I managed to track down Clark at his production company in southern California. I told his secretary I had these two versions of the story, and I had a compulsive need to get things right. Could Clark just tell me which was right?

Several calls later, she told me she had caught up with Clark and he just didn't want to talk about it anymore. "I've heard the story several times," she said. "Dick says he doesn't care what goes in your book, one way or the other."

Oh, well I think we can say without fear of successful contradiction that Dick Clark had a psychic experience that day in Philadelphia.

11
DID HOUDINI COME BACK TO SAY HELLO TO HIS WIDOW?

Harry Houdini was probably the greatest magician—at least the most publicized one—of the twentieth century. He was also known as a relentless exposer of fraudulent psychics and mediums.

In the 1920s, he had ample scope for this activity. As a result of the slaughter of World War I, plus the postwar flu epidemic, millions of people had taken untimely leave of this vale, and the millions left behind were eager to contact them. Séances abounded, and some of them were inevitably presided over by phony mediums.

As cynical observers of Houdini's campaign were quick to point out, the great magician reaped a rich harvest of publicity from his medium-busting. Some magicians are still winning newsprint and TV appearances by assuring the media there is no such thing as the psychic. But it would be a mistake to assume that Houdini had no belief at all in the occult. In his youth,

he performed as a phony psychic with his wife, Beatrice, as his assistant. It is said that Houdini dropped
this act in some consternation when evidence of true
psychic phenomena began to occur during his performances. This, tradition has it, made him quite uneasy,
and he switched to honest magic.

Among firmly recorded evidence of Houdini's interest in the occult is his endorsement of Alexander Martin, a well-known psychic photographer. Martin, Scot-
tish-born, came to the American West and began
getting his first paranormal pictures in 1879. He took
tintypes of babies in the mining town of Blackhawk,
Colorado, and discovered extra images of children who
were not visibly present. Early in the twentieth century,
Sir Arthur Conan Doyle, creator of Sherlock Holmes
and a devoted investigator of the occult, visited Martin
and termed him "one of the greatest spirit photographers in the world." Doyle, however, was considered by
some hard-nosed investigators to be lamentably soft-
nosed; in fact, many observers felt the father of the
great detective was taken in by fake psychic performances that should not fool a retarded six-year-old.

Houdini was not about to take Doyle's word on
Martin; he went to see the photographer himself. This
visit has been recorded many times, and it's summa-
rized well in an article on Martin, called therein "the
dean of Colorado photographers," in the September 12,
1971, issue of the *Denver Post*:

"In 1915, Harry Houdini, the master magician,
made a trip to Denver to determine in his own mind,
once and for all, whether there was anything to the
spirit pictures. . . . Photographs were taken and Houdini was quoted as saying he witnessed every step of the

Harry Houdini

process. The magician said he was amazed when he saw several ghostly figures on the finished plates. 'I am thoroughly convinced that he [Martin] has the ability to capture the spirit world on film,' Houdini said. 'I observed him closely under the most exact test conditions and the results are nothing short of miraculous. I believe Alexander Martin to be honest and his craft authentic.' "

According to a short account in *Arthur Ford: The Man Who Talked with the Dead,* by Allen Spraggett and William V. Rauscher, Houdini's friend Joseph Dunninger, a mentalist of some fame, told of a peculiar photograph taken under Houdini's supervision in a Los Angeles Spiritualist church in 1923. The book states:

"Of ten photographs taken, one showed a strange, luminous streak with a blob at the top—a little imagination could construe it as a facsimile of a human form—for which no explanation was ever found. Houdini claimed to have ruled out all normal causes, such as a scratch on the negative, and offered a thousand-dollar reward to anyone who could duplicate the phenomenon under the same conditions. Apparently nobody did."

I phoned Spraggett at his home near Toronto for further information, and he said, "Houdini had read of a medium's dying, and her saying she would prove the existence of afterlife at her funeral. She said she would make every effort to appear. And the luminous streak stood about five and a half feet high behind the casket where she said she would appear. Several people in the group said they could see her clairvoyantly. Houdini saw nothing, but when they developed the picture there it was. The guy who developed the plates in Houdini's presence was a known crony of Houdini's who probably didn't believe anything, so he certainly wouldn't have tampered with it. Houdini was in the darkroom with him, and later swore out an affidavit that this was a genuine phenomenon and that he had not contrived to create it in any way, that he had not expected it, and that he could not explain it under the circumstances."

But whatever publicity sprang from Houdini's "ripping the muslin," as he put it, from fake mediums pales in comparison to his fiercely debated return in

1929, almost three years after his death. Acres of news-print, as well as books—pro, con, and undecided—have been written about this event, a fitting epitaph to a life devoted to mystery.

The other actor in this extravaganza was, appropriately, as well known a medium as Houdini had been a magician. Arthur Ford was possibly the best—certainly the most publicized—psychic of his time. From most accounts Ford had extraordinary psychic powers; he proved them again and again, usually in public. At the time of the Houdini episode, Ford was pastor of New York's First Spiritualist Church. Ford purported to work through a spirit guide he called Fletcher, whom he said was a childhood friend who was killed in World War I.

When Houdini died he was as obsessed with the hereafter as ever. According to his wife, known to friends as Bess, he told her on his deathbed that he would try to return with a message and gave her the message. Bess offered a ten-thousand-dollar reward to the person who could bring through this message. However, after being deluged by hopeful message-bearers of every description, most of them seemingly on the fringe of insanity, she withdrew the offer.

Then in January of 1928, Arthur Ford announced that through Fletcher he had received a message from Houdini's mother. It consisted of one word: "Forgive." Bess expressed great excitement on hearing of the message. She said for many years that Houdini had hoped to receive this message from his dead mother. This fervent desire was occasioned by the fact that during the latter years of his life Houdini had refused to speak to his brother Leopold. Sadie, the wife of a third brother, Nathan, had left her husband to marry Leopold.

This was not the way things were done in a close-knit Jewish family (Houdini's real name was Ehrich Weiss). But Houdini sometimes had second thoughts about snubbing his brother and yearned for advice from his mother.

This message created something of a furor, until it was noted by Doyle, among others—that Bess had disclosed the word a year before to a reporter for the Brooklyn *Eagle* and it had been printed in that paper.

In other parts of her message, Houdini's mother purportedly said, "Since this message has come through it will open the channel for the other." And as the months went on, Ford came up with what he said was the first word of a two-word message Houdini had promised his wife. That word was "Rosabelle."

This was correct, said Bess, and on January 7, 1929, Ford held a séance at her home, at which the second word supposedly came through: "Believe."

This message from the other world seems to have kept America amply supplied with breakfast conversation until the crash of the stock market a few months later provided something more immediate to talk about. For a time, no respectable newspaper could let many issues pass without a resounding feature story on the matter, and no self-respecting editorial writer could duck doing a think piece, even though most of them sat gingerly but determinedly on the fence.

The New York *Graphic* insisted stridently that Ford and Bess were in cahoots. Two facts prevented general acceptance of this view: one, the *Graphic* was the yellowest of yellow journals and tended to avoid the truth when falsification would sell more papers or, it sometimes seemed, would just be more fun; and two, the *Graphic*'s women's editor, Rea Jaure, the epitome of the 1920s sob sister, and Bess had had a bitter falling out on another matter and cordially hated each other. And so, Houdini's return faded from public consciousness, remembered mostly by historians, magicians, and devotees of the psychic, who divided pretty much on sectarian lines.

Ford died in 1971, and soon afterward Spraggett and Rauscher, two of his close friends, set about writing a definitive biography. It was to be something of a memorial. Spraggett was a well-known Canadian spiritualist and writer, and Rauscher was the rector of an Episcopal church in Woodbury, New Jersey. Rauscher not only had written several books on the occult, but he was a magician who had worked his way through college by doing a magic act. Rauscher spoke at Ford's funeral service and was Ford's literary legatee.

The two writers had access to documents that had never been available during the medium's lifetime. They were in for a shock. They found obituary after obituary in Ford's files, as well as other documents that could freshen Ford's inspiration if Fletcher's were to flag. Spraggett and Rauscher found themselves in a peculiar position. They were preparing a book to be titled *Arthur Ford: The Man Who Talked with the Dead*, and here they were unearthing evidence that he didn't always seem to do that. They had little doubt that his communications with the other world were *usually* valid—but not, it would seem, *always*. This situation is not uncommon among even the most authentic of psychics; they are human as well as psychic, with the usual human arrogance, ego tripping, and intermittent cupidity.

But, stout-hearted men, Spraggett and Rauscher pressed on. They wrote the book, but included their discovery of Ford's occasional chicanery with an aside to the effect, "So who's perfect?" But in their chapter on Houdini, they strongly espoused the validity of the messages. The book was published in 1973. When I spoke with Spraggett in 1987, he still seemed staunchly on Ford's side. Some Ford detractors had complained the code word used by Houdini was a common magicians' code, known to innumerable people. Spraggett didn't put much stock in that ploy.

"What was known among magicians was the code," he told me, "but what was not known were the two words that were to be transmitted in the code. There's a hell of a difference between knowing the code and knowing the message. I might know the Morse code, but if I don't know the two words it doesn't help me very much."

Rauscher, however, took a different tack. In 1975, he published *The Spiritual Frontier,* a book in which he discussed the Houdini matter in an addendum.

"After the publication of Arthur Ford's biography," he wrote, "I received a letter from a man named Jay Abbott, who said he could shed some interesting light on the Houdini affair."

Abbott, it turned out, had known both Ford and Bess well. He was, in fact, a believer in spiritualism, but he had some startling things to tell Rauscher. To quote Rauscher's book:

"They were close friends, he said; in fact, 'she was in

love with Ford.' He told me that they frequently dated before the famous séance . . . Jay Abbott said that the night before the séance at which Arthur brought through the code message, he [Ford] and Beatrice were out dancing and both stumbled, and she hurt herself. This, said Abbott, was the 'fall' that Mrs. Houdini suffered that was mentioned in the newspaper accounts of the séance."

Bess told reporters that she had fallen down some stairs.

Abbott told Rauscher he didn't think Bess had conspired with Ford; she had been duped by the highly attractive medium. But that's anybody's guess. It doesn't happen to be Rauscher's. He told me:

"My contention is that Arthur Ford and Bess were in cahoots and that it was a grand and glorious hoax. It was real ragtime. Ford never spoke of these things. I once asked him if he had any feelings about the Houdini case at this point. He was smoking a cigar and looking out the window, and he said, 'Well, only I know, don't I? All the rest of them are dead.' "

12
JOHN LENNON DOESN'T SEEM TO HAVE LEFT

When he was alive, John Lennon rarely did things the conventional way. He was the wildest of the Beatles. He once put in the hospital a music critic who suggested that he and Brian Epstein, the Beatles' manager, were having a homosexual affair. Lennon was a close friend of Epstein's, but he could be casually cruel. He once offered a title for Epstein's autobiography: *Queer Jew*.

When Lennon and Paul McCartney, who founded the Beatles with him, first got together in their native Liverpool, McCartney's family was somewhat appalled. To quote Lennon:

"Everyone said, 'Oh, that John, you know he is a bad influence on Paul and that Paul is such a good little boy. But then after he met John.' That attitude."

"Were they right?" he was asked.

"That is probably correct," he replied.

The Dakota, where John Lennon lived   *(photo by Arthur Myers)*

The operative fact about this exchange is that it purportedly occurred in 1983, three years after Lennon was shot to death in the doorway of his New York apartment building.

The questioner was Paul Zuromski, editor of *Psychic Guide* magazine (now retitled *Body/Mind/Spirit*), speaking through a medium, Bill Tenuto.

Is this for real?

Lennon seems to be creating physical manifestations all over the planet. He also seems to be communicating through countless people. A mind-boggling concept, but as the testimony mounts, a researcher's mind begins to boggle at a slower rate, and he begins to pay increasingly closer attention.

For example, Bill Tenuto is a New Jersey–born man

in his thirties, a professional with degrees in sociology from the University of Notre Dame and New York University. He told me he became psychic a few years ago in an intriguing way; he was in bed with a woman who had been studying tantra yoga, an approach to mysticism that involves sex. Tenuto did not know his bed partner was employing this manner of exploring the infinite until he suddenly found himself out of his body. He then began studying seriously with psychics.

During a class taught by highly regarded California psychic Katie MacPherson, Lennon supposedly started speaking through Tenuto, a process that is sometimes called channeling. Since then Tenuto supposedly has had many sessions with Lennon and most have been taped. I am no Henry Higgins, but the accent sounds reasonably Liverpudlian to my untrained ears.

In writing this book, since I am not particularly psychic, I sometimes felt rather helplessly dependent on the authenticity of what people told me—people who said they were psychic, or who just professed to be witnesses. So it was reassuring when something happened to give me an indication that something genuine was indeed going on.

About four months after I interviewed Bill Tenuto over the phone, I saw him in action. It was at a symposium in New York under the auspices of *Psychic Guide* magazine. Tenuto was one of the speakers. He is a short man, with an unassuming manner. He announced that he was going into a trance, and probably would be channeling Lennon, among others. Something certainly seemed to be happening. It is said that everyone has psychic abilities, but the only one I am aware of in myself is seeing auras, by the simple method of letting

Bill Tenuto, who claims to channel John Lennon
(photo by Arthur Myers)

my eyes go out of focus. While Tenuto was in a trance, I saw a gigantic purple aura around him, ballooning out about a yard. In fact, it seemed to envelope him. I saw him through flashes and ribbons of purple. Other people in the audience saw the same thing. It is said that purple in the aura denotes spirituality, so it might well seem that Tenuto was doing something very spiritual.

Channeling Lennon seems to have become a widespread activity. Books have been published by people who claim to have contacted him. One, called—in no uncertain terms—*John Lennon Conversations*, by psychic Linda Deer Domnitz, opens with the following words:

"No one could have been more taken by surprise than I on the day of December 8, 1980, when John

Lennon was killed. I was even more shocked four days later when. . . John Lennon's spirit appeared in the room and proceeded to speak to me."

Domnitz called me from Arizona—I live near Boston—one morning while I was working on this chapter. At the moment of her call, I was casting about for a good transition from the psychic indications that Lennon might still be around to the content of his messages. What she said when I picked up the phone fit in perfectly with what I was writing. I said half jokingly that maybe Lennon was at work. She laughed and said, "Just as you said this, a light over my table that has been dead for days went on. He does these things all the time."

Domnitz told me that a number of people have reported psychic manifestations involving Lennon while they were reading her book. Some have seen apparitions of him, she said. She told of an experience related to her by a friend, Robert Shields, who lives in the same town as she does, Sedona, Arizona. Shields is a mime who has appeared on TV with such performers as Bob Hope and Red Skelton. He is a protégé of Marcel Marceau and has won Emmy awards for television productions. He took Domnitz's book to India and was reading it while sitting in an airport. Domnitz said:

"He said, 'John, if this is really you, do something to prove it to me.' At that moment, his left shoulder jerked forward. He said, 'That's OK, but I want something more significant.' And he said at that moment John knocked him off his chair in the airport. The same thing happened the next day when he asked for another demonstration. His left shoulder jerked forward, and he asked for more. Then he heard John's voice, in his

Doorway of the Dakota, where John Lennon was shot
(photo by Arthur Myers)

accent, saying, 'Oh, give me a break, Robert. What do you want me to do, appear on the ceiling?' "

A young man and woman in the Boston area, who prefer to remain anonymous, also claim to be channeling Lennon. I sat with them one evening as they were supposedly doing this. The young woman appeared to go into a trance and began to speak with somewhat of a Liverpool accent. I later listened to tapes of the young man's channeling, and the accent was much stronger, more on the order of the Tenuto tapes.

I came loaded for bear. By this time I had done several weeks of research on Lennon and knew a few esoteric facts about him. I asked tricky questions and

got correct answers. I may possibly have experienced a
first in my long journalistic career: I may have interviewed a ghost.

Could these young people also have done research,
preparing to have their claims tested? I doubt it. They
seemed to be very sincere and spiritual. And insisting
on anonymity as they did, they hardly seemed to be
courting notoriety.

As we sat in the young woman's living room, she
began shaking her head slowly, then mumbling, then
speaking. Lennon—if it were indeed him—was a most
courteous and considerate interviewee. He seemed to
want to be in this book to spread what he considers his
message. He seemed to realize that I intended a bit of a
cross examination but was not resentful. In fact, he
invited questions.

I asked him what he thought of Bill Harry. Harry is
a British music writer with whom I had been in touch
several times. He is author of *The Book of Lennon*.
They knew each other as children in Liverpool, and
Lennon did some of his first writing for *Mersey Beat*, a
magazine edited by Harry.

"Do you have a message for Bill Harry?" I asked.

"He's doing good work," was the reply.

I asked what was his relationship with Harry.

"We knew each other," was the reply. "We were
acquaintances. We'd see each other in the hallways of
the school."

I asked if Tenuto's tapes were legitimate.

"Oh yes," was the reply. "Bill and I are working out
some problems we've had. We did some good, strong
work together for a couple of years and then had, I
guess, kind of a falling-out. He was disappointed that

he couldn't get his book published and kind of lost faith in me."

This corresponded with what Tenuto had told me. Tenuto said he sometimes wondered whether he was making it all up. "I became exhausted and very disillusioned when I couldn't get the book published," Tenuto told me. "I'm not certain it was John Lennon. But Katie [MacPherson] insists it was John Lennon, that I'm too good a medium for it not to have been, and that I couldn't possibly have dictated the kind of material that is in the book by myself. I'm not that clever. All of this contributes to my wanting to get away from John Lennon, but he still comes around once in a while."

This jibed with what MacPherson had told me. "Bill is beginning to wonder if he made all this up," she said. "He's really beating himself up over that." she added, "If anybody asks for any proof of John, John can become very foul-mouthed." (I must have caught him on a good night—assuming it was not the young woman herself, or a more gentle departed spirit, doing a masquerade.)

"I came to know John on a personal level," MacPherson said of her experiences in working with him through Tenuto. "I'm a therapist. I've done a lot of work with him. I did five therapy sessions with him. I've helped some spirits."

(More and more astonishing! The dead can not only be interviewed by inquisitive writers; they can also be treated by psychotherapists! What would Freud have thought of this? He might have loved it. He is said to have remarked that if he had his life to live over he would devote it to parapsychology rather than psychology. And, of course, Jung was very much a mystic.)

The Beatles: Paul, Ringo, John, and George

MacPherson continued: "John felt that he was sent here to get the world ready for world peace and that he didn't make it. I tried to get John to let go of the anger that dominated this lifetime. His mother abandoned him. The anger started then and grew in this lifetime. Bill is just as filled with anger about his early life as John is. It's no mystery why the two of them are so much on the same wavelength."

On the night I attended the séance held by the two young people, I asked about MacPherson.

"Yes," was the reply, "she can tune in to me whenever she wants to. When she wants to, she does."

I asked about Paul Zuromski, and the reply was: "Yes, he was the fellow who talked to me through Bill. He's head of a magazine. I've had quite a few conversations with him."

I asked about Domintz. "She was one of the first channels I started coming through after I passed over," was the reply. "I was still new at it."

Is her book legitimate?

"Oh yes," was the reply.

Harry had told me, by transatlantic telephone, that he was researching an article on the constant reports that Lennon was appearing to people or channeling through them. He generously shared some of his research. Harry said that Yoko Ono, Lennon's widow, wanted to marry again but was waiting for John's permission. I asked "Lennon" about this.

"Not to be impolite," he said gently, "but that's none of your business."

Harry had also told me of reports that Yoko had seen John sitting at his white piano in their apartment. Sometimes the bench was pushed back, and sometimes John's spirit spoke to her. I asked about this.

"Yeah," was the reply, "I talk to her and she talks to me. She's got a couple of psychics she uses to channel that we talk through. Yeah, I'm around her a lot."

He spoke about his channeling appearances in general. "People think of me. I was famous. If someone feels very strongly about me and the way I died, and thinks about me and sends me love, then that works like a magnet with me. It pulls me toward them, and if they're perceptive and they're open then they'll see me, because I'm there. But a lot of that goes on unconsciously, you know. Not only for them but for me too. It's only recently that I've been able to keep track of all the different ones."

New York psychic Shawn Robbins, who does work for the *National Enquirer,* told me about a time she had gone on assignment to the Dakota with a reporter and photographer. "The story idea," she said, "was to contact or see the ghost of John Lennon outside the Dakota. It was about one in the afternoon, in the spring of 1985. At a distance, physically, I could see energy waves, like a body. I saw it where he was shot. He was worried that there would be a fire in the Dakota involving Yoko Ono's apartment and he wanted to get that idea across. I've seen Lennon's spirit outside the Dakota at other times, too, When I'm on the West Side, sometimes I'll go by there out of curiosity and some-times I see a fleeting image that looks like John Len-non."

The *Enquirer* and other supermarket tabloids have run stories about Lennon being sighted outside the Dakota. One supposed witness is John Ludlum, who works in a music store near the Dakota. Another is Gail Smith, who also works nearby. Joey Harrow, a musi-cian who lives nearby, and Amanda Moores, a writer, together claim to have seen Lennon's ghost outside the Dakota.

When I asked "Lennon" about this, the reply was, "Oh yes, sure. Yoko's there, Sean [their son] is there, so of course I'm there with them a lot because I'm still working so closely with the Earth. So anyone who is receptive would be able to tune in on me."

Harry had told me of reports that while he was living Lennon had seen a resident ghost at the Dakota, the "crying lady." I asked about this.

"Yes," was the reply, "it was in the hallway, outside my door. I came out one day and felt this weirdness around. I saw it in sort of the corner of my eye. I thought I saw it but I wasn't quite sure. But then someone told me later about the ghost."

The Dakota is an intriguing place, probably best known as the setting for the spooky film *Rosemary's Baby*. Many famous people live there. When I called the superintendent's office, for example, a clerk I reached spoke aside to someone to say, "That package is for Lauren Bacall." Incidentally, he said he had not seen Lennon's ghost.

Twenty years ago, while writing for *Coronet* magazine, I spent a week in actor Robert Ryan's apartment interviewing him for an article. I was highly intrigued when Harry mentioned that Lennon and Yoko had moved into that very apartment. Both of them were interested in the psychic and spiritual, and they supposedly had contacted Ryan and his wife, both of whom were dead. I asked about this.

"Yeah, that happened," was the reply. "Yoko and I used to have psychics over. We were very into the occult. We didn't know whether to believe it or not. Ryan was hanging around, and a psychic picked up on him, that he was there, watching what was going on, that he was attracted to us. He liked what we were doing. He liked the energy that we had given to the building. But there wasn't much of a connection between us; there wasn't any special need to communicate."

Many people reported having a paranormal experience concerning Lennon the night of his death. One is Barbara Garwell, who says Lennon appeared at the foot of her bed in England at the moment he was shot in New York. Garwell has a good track record in parapsychology. She works with Dr. Keith Hearne, a parapsychologist who has compiled a massive dossier on premonitions. "She is my star subject," he says.

At the time of Lennon's death, Bob Freeman, photographer for many of the Beatles' album covers, was living in Hong Kong. Freeman has said that the day before John's death, John's picture, hanging on the wall of his apartment, fell to the floor. I asked "Lennon" about that.

"That sort of thing happens," was the reply. "Not to have an ego about it, but it [his death] was a big event. There were reverberations and manifestations around the world."

Apropos of this, at the *Psychic Guide* symposium I met Eugenia Macer-Story, who said she was psychic and who told me of an experience she claimed to have had with the spirit of the French dramatist Molière (see following chapter). Another time she told me of an experience she had the night Lennon died:

"I saw a very clear apparition of Lennon in my mind's eye, and I thought it was a friend of mine who resembles him and I became very concerned about my friend—then later on I found out John Lennon had been killed. I saw somebody in a dark pea coat. When I get impressions they're very visual. I got socked in the solar plexus with this feeling of fear that I get when I know somebody has been hurt or is in serious trouble. When I heard the eleven o'clock news I discovered that he'd been shot. I was debilitated; I told my friends that I couldn't speak on the telephone.

"The impression I got that evening is the terror when somebody has been badly hurt or dies suddenly, when it's just pain and terror and not knowing what to do. I would imagine if someone was very mentally gifted before he died and he was killed suddenly in that way, being that there's no time or space, the mental entity would just go wherever it perceived a place to actualize. Lots of people have that experience when there is so much disorientation and terror in the spirit that it just goes to anyone who happens to be empathetic to it."

Eugenia is a poet, and she wrote a poem that was published in the Woodstock, New York, *Times*: It reads, in part:

Premonition of the Death of John Lennon

last night   fear from nowhere hit my gut
                sobbing through my body like hurt
                osciloscope energy
I thought it was the new drifter from L.A. in
                trouble again
                or—a funeral passed down the
                block—some lost
anonymous spirit finding haven along my nerves
                I called Harry. I said: someone's
                going to die.
He asked: who is it?   I said: a friend.
                Don't make me tell it. Just a man
Dark haired in an ordinary overcoat
                Standing outside a hotel door . . .
                John Lennon, Famous singer   as
                in life
you found words for the dumb cry "enough. . .
                now; enough now. peace. we've had
                enough."
I walk the streets of bedlam
                playing my banjo like a crazy nerve
putting my quarter into the TILT machine
                where the songs come up absurd.

Another account of an occult marking of Lennon's death appeared in an article by James Crenshaw in the April 1987 *Fate* magazine. In his article "Psychic Adventure in Beverly Hills." Crenshaw wrote of a woman who with her family encountered a variety of strange incidents after going to California and moving into a new house. One of them involved Lennon. Crenshaw quoted the woman as follows:

"It was daytime and the date was December 9, 1980, the day after John Lennon's senseless murder outside his New York apartment.

"The news reports were very disturbing to me, not because I was a great Beatles fan but because of the meaningless violence of John Lennon's death. I turned off the TV with all its details of the murder and sat rocking in my rocking chair, contemplating the meaning of life and death. Was there an answer to acts like this?

"We had stacked several sets of record albums against a wall in the living room. Each set of albums was maybe seven or eight inches thick, standing on end and side by side. At the moment I was not aware of these as I continued my meditation.

"I was thinking many in the psychic field believe that life goes on. If so, where is John Lennon now? What would he say if he could speak to those he left behind? Perhaps it would be an important message he would like to get across. I knew in my mind I was just fooling around but I thought, with everything that had happened, I might just tune in to see what I could experience. Probably nothing would happen.

"Nevertheless, I concentrated on John Lennon, saying to myself, 'If you're here, and there is something you want to say about what happened or any other message, please know that I am willing to do my part.'

"I suddenly heard a noise in the corner of the room. Opening my eyes, I turned around and saw a stack of albums falling forward one by one, very slowly, as if someone were intentionally looking through them. None of these albums had ever fallen before. I could see the titles on each album as they fell, until the falling stopped. I was shocked; the falling albums had stopped at the only Beatles album in the stack.

"What caught my eye was a picture of the four Beatles; from the cover John Lennon was looking straight at me. I stared back in disbelief; then it struck me! There before me was the personal message I had sought—the title. It said it all in words as loud as if they were spoken: *Let it be*."

According to *National Enquirer* columnist Neil Blincow, Paul McCartney has said he has more than once seen Lennon at the foot of his bed, smiling. In some channeling sessions, "Lennon" has said he has also been in touch with George Harrison. I asked him at the Boston séance if he had been in touch with the Beatles' drummer, Ringo Starr, and the reply was enigmatic: "That's something you'll have to ask Ringo. I don't like to say anything more about that."

In another column, Blincow told of manifestations that supposedly occurred in a radio studio in London during a tribute to Lennon on the fourth anniversary of his death. The power reportedly went out in the studio for fifteen minutes. Disc jockey Peter Powell is quoted as saying over the air, "This is incredible—I feel like Lennon is here." Another deejay said it felt as though the temperature had plunged twenty degrees,

which sometimes happens during psychic manifestations. According to Blincow's column, "Powell was so
moved that he left the studio, unable to finish the
program."

The supposed spirit of Lennon is philosophical
about the manner of his death and forgiving of his
assassin, Mark David Chapman. Lennon has said in
other séances the murder was a matter of karma; he and
Chapman knew each other in an earlier incarnation,
and he "owed" Chapman a death. I asked about this in
the séance I attended. The reply was that this was true.

"What happened that he would shoot you?" I asked.

"What do you think? If you had to guess, what
would it be?"

"I would say that you shot him."

"I didn't shoot him."

"But you killed him?"

"Yes. We were in a fight. It was a stupid thing."

"Where was it?"

"I want to say Germany. I didn't mean to kill him,
but it happened. But I want to say that I don't hold any
grudge against him. I don't hold any bad feelings. It
happened as it was meant to happen."

Rosemary Brown, the musical medium and the subject of two chapters in this book, wrote in her third
book *Look Beyond Tomorrow*, that Lennon has come
to her.

"He looks," she wote, "as he must have done at the
height of the Beatles' success. He was clean-shaven,
fresh-faced, and without glasses. He told me he bears
no malice against his murderer, Mark Chapman. He
knows the man is mad. He is just sorry that his death

caused so much sorrow and suffering to his wife, Yoko, and son Sean.''

She said that Lennon wants his elder son, Julian, who has had considerable success as a performer, to perform the compositions he passes on to Brown.

In Lennon's youth, as noted at the beginning of this chapter, he was a rough customer. In a channeling with Tenuto, there is this passage:

"In me younger days, I was rebellious to the point of being almost obnoxious. I look back on that now and I understand it better, much better than I did then. It was a convenient weapon for me to use in terms of keeping myself isolated from other people so I wouldn't let anybody get too close in, do you know what I mean?''

The March/April 1985 issue of the *Saturday Review* contained a review of a new book about Lennon that spoke to this aspect of Lennon in no uncertain terms. The book was published in the United States under the title *Lennon*. The author is Ray Coleman, who knew the Beatles in their Liverpool days. He himself is from Liverpool. Coleman wrote:

"He was brilliant, warm, tender, sensitive and generous. He was also infuriating, tough, aggressive, naïve, and woundingly abrasive. He bruised many victims, sometimes physically, often verbally. But even to have been tongue-lashed by Lennon was fame of a kind.''

Coleman wrote of the young Lennon's penchant for sick humor. At school, Lennon was depicted as ridiculing cripples and crudely insulting his classmates, traits that continued even when the Beatles began touring. "He was very sick,'' recalled singer Helen Shapiro, who toured with the Beatles, "especially if he saw a couple of nuns going by. He'd pull the crudest faces at them.''

Coleman quoted Michael Isaacson, who attended art school with Lennon: "I think if he had not become successful, he may well have become a really nasty piece of work."

But something happened along the way. He mellowed, expanded, and met Yoko Ono; he wrote and performed important music and lyrics. He and Yoko worked hard for world peace, planning peace festivals and working with radicals such as Abbie Hoffman and Jerry Rubin. The Nixon White House made a long and unsuccessful effort to deport him, citing his earlier conviction on drug possession charges in England.

"He's continued to work for world peace," Domnitz told me. "He's this giant battery that we can tune in to—not only to get information from him and draw energy from him, but also to link us up with everyone else on the planet, that is, everyone connected to him. This is a big network of people. He's inspiring us all the time and tuning us into our oneness. He's not appearing just for the sake of psychic phenomena. It's a very serious thing. We're all channels, we're all mediums, we can all receive this information."

The purported spirit of Lennon said on the Tenuto tapes:

"I died at just the right time, when I was supposed to do this next step of my evolution, to do this next phase of my work. I haven't missed a beat. It's just the next step. Everything just fits in, and I'm a piece to the puzzle. It's for my own progression, and through that I also make a contribution to the rest of the world. So get the bloody message, everybody, won't you? When we all get that message there won't be any bombs, there won't be any wars, there won't be people maneuvering for power, people lusting after this or lusting after that, getting greedy to have more than they need. Everybody will get what they want, there's plenty for everybody, there's an infinite supply of everything once people get the message just to do what they came here to do. When you're doing what feels right to you, you're doing what you came here to do.

"God is everything, you see. God is each of us. We are of God and God is in us. God is you, that's the message. One day everybody is going to realize that the physical existence of living is designed to force them to awaken. It's designed to bring them to enlightenment, to bring them into the light, to the awareness that they are light. The whole physical world is nothing but a chain of illusions, a collection of pictures. It's all sort of like a camouflage, it's not the ultimate reality at all. It springs from ultimate reality, but it's not reality.

"So rock on, everybody. Live your lives. I wish you well, I wish you peace, I wish you love, I wish for you whatever it is you're asking for. And I bless you all. I get to do that, man, because I'm a spirit, eh?"

13
IS THAT MOLIÈRE HANGING ABOUT IN THE WINGS?

The story in this chapter has very little evidentiality; it hangs completely on the subjective experience of one person. There are no witnesses, no knowledge that could have been acquired only by supernormal means, none of the buttressing so dear to the hearts of we who write—or read—about the parapsychological. Because it is interesting nevertheless, I have included it here.

This is what happened.

Recently, Eugenia Macer-Story from Woodstock, New York, got in touch with me. A psychic, her card carries the words ADVICE AND INVESTIGATIONS. She told me she had worked in police investigations and in cases involving espionage.

She is also a poet and a playwright, and many of her plays have been performed off-off-Broadway and in regional theater.

Eugenia Macer-Story
(photo by Arthur Myers)

Macer-Story has a master's degree in theater from Columbia University, and she still keeps in touch with her favorite professor, Albert Bermel. Bermel is a Molière scholar. He has translated thirteen of Molière's plays and is writing an analysis of the great French dramatist's work.

When I spoke to Bermel, he was unsure about endorsing what Eugenia said happened to her; he said he had no way of knowing. But he was high on her as a person and as a writer. "She's an enormously gifted poet and playwright," he told me. "She also calls herself a witch, and she's involved with ESP and UFOs and various other phenomena of that kind. She's a very astute and unusual person."

The events began, Eugenia told me, when she was living near Salem, Massachusetts, with her then-husband, who worked on computers. During the Bicentennial she opened a store called Magik Mirror, apparently a blend of 1976 patriotism and the occult.

One day a young man came into her store, giving the name of Carroll Rockwood. He had come to Salem from the Northwest, and said he had received directions during an occult ceremony that he was to contact a witch. What better place to find one than Salem? Eugenia gave him a reading.

"As I began to speak to him," she says, "I began to have the impression he had something to do with Molière, or that Molière was present."

A spirit came through, she says, that identified itself as Jean-Baptiste Poquelin, which was Molière's real name. She said the spirit insisted on being addressed by his correct name, rather than the stage name Molière.

"Later that evening, after Rockwood left," Macer-Story continues, "I began to have unusual thoughts about Molière. At that time I was not working on anything related to Molière-like material. Imagine my consternation to be flooded with the impression that Carroll Rockwood in a previous lifetime had been the mistress of JBP. He had been an actress who was selfish and difficult. The spirit was communicating to me that Carroll had been a woman named Madeleine, and that he had a negative destiny in this present lifetime because he had been unfaithful to JBP in the seventeenth century."

Although she has a master's degree in theater, Eugenia told me she knew very little about Molière. All her life she had had an inexplicable antipathy toward things French. "Since childhood," she says, "I have had an aversion to the French language, and had refused to learn French in school. I had, when a child, the idea that things which were French were decadent or warped. This amounted to a phobia. It kept me away from any literature or art that was French. This lasted till about seven years ago."

She began to correspond with Bermel, who was able to confirm many of the things she felt were coming through about Molière and about the period of King Louis XIV in general.

For example, Molière had a long-term relationship with a successful actress named Madeleine Bejart, who acted in his company, and who some scholars say originally persuaded the young man to take to the theater. Some twenty years later, Molière married Armande Bejart, Madeleine's sister, although Molière's enemies said she was her daughter.

As time went on, Eugenia says, "I began to receive messages about that era in history, and about Molière. One of the messages I received was that this was the spirit of Molière, which was unquiet because he wasn't buried in consecrated ground, and also because he had been involved with what we would call witchcraft during his lifetime.' He wished to communicate with me because I had also lived during that time."

It is true that Molière, whose satirical comedy *Tartuffe* took the clergy to task and caused a considerable scandal in France, was buried without ceremony or without receiving the sacraments.

"I began," Eugenia says, "to get communications that were very dark. I began to see scenes of a dungeon and all kinds of fearful images."

Eugenia suspects these images may be connected with an unfortunate man named Nicholas Fourquet. Fourquet was superintendent of the Finances of France

in the first days of Louis XIV. He had the bad judgment to build a castle, called Vaux-le-Vicomte, that was
so beautiful that the king became jealous. The king
had been invited to the opening of the castle, and
Molière had written a new play that was performed at
this magnificent party. But Vaux-le-Vicomte came to
life for only one glorious evening. Three weeks later,
the King had Fourquet thrown into the first of the
dungeons in which he was to spend the rest of his life.
He died, fifteen years later, in a dark dungeon in the
gloomy, wind-buffeted fortress of Pignerol, in the Alps.

Fourquet had, early in Molière's career, been a pa-
tron of the young dramatist. Eugenia said she felt some
kind of connection with these people and thought that
some members of the group were involved in black
magic. And that, she says, is why she has constant
telepathic impressions of that three-hundred-year-old,
faraway milieu.

As I've said, obviously, none of this is evidential.
One has to accept Eugenia's word about the messages,
and also that she, a dramatist with a master's degree in
theater, knew very little about Molière, France's most
celebrated playwright. But if this is all true, she was
getting some very interesting messages.

14
MONKEYS IN THE CLOSET
(BEATRICE STRAIGHT)

Beatrice Straight is an actress who won an Academy Award for her performance in the film *Network* and a Tony for her part in *The Crucible*, Arthur Miller's play set in Salem during the witchcraft hysteria.

Her house, in the Berkshire Hills of western Massachusetts, seems to be haunted, with whispers in the night and other offbeat phenomena. Her most intriguing encounter with the spirit world, however, happened several years ago when she was living in a house that had been owned by her parents, in Old Westbury, Long Island.

She and her husband, Peter Cookson, an actor and producer, were using the house as a weekend retreat from Manhattan. Some time before, he had produced and she had appeared in a Broadway production called *The Innocents*, a play about ghosts adapted by William

Archibald from Henry James's spooky story, *Turn of the Screw*.

Beatrice comes from a wealthy and distinguished family. Her father, Willard, was trained as an architect at Cornell University. After his death, his wife put up a building at Cornell called Willard Straight Hall. The Straights were founders of *The New Republic* and *Theater Arts Monthly*. Her brother, Michael, was the editor of *The New Republic* for a long time.

Her father served as U.S. Consul in Manchuria. When he returned to the United States he brought many things back from China, with which he furnished parts of the house and grounds. A Chinese garden and a Chinese room were features of the estate.

Willard Straight died during World War I. Beatrice recalled that through the years there was something strange about the bedroom he had once used.

"People didn't like to sleep in it," she says, "although it was a perfectly ordinary room. My husband said the room had a weird feeling. My mother-in-law wouldn't sleep in there because her dog always barked whenever he was in that room."

One evening in the 1950s, Beatrice and her husband brought some friends out to the Long Island house for the weekend. Among them was Archibald, who had an interest in the occult. In the evening, by which time no one was feeling much pain, he suggested doing some table tipping. Eagerly falling in with the idea, the group trooped off to the Chinese room. The tables wouldn't work there, so they went up to the former bedroom of Willard Straight. Beatrice related the events to me:

"Bill Archibald told us what to do, that the table

Beatrice Straight

would tip and tap out letters. [For example, one tip equals an A, five tips equals an E.] So we sat around a small table with our hands on top, and it suddenly started to go like mad, tipping and all.

"It said it was a spirit from the Gobi Desert. At one

point, there were only two of us with our hands on top of the table, and it raised above our heads and was shaking, and crashed. Before the night was over, we broke two tables that way. The second table spelled out 'monkeys in the closet.'

"I went to the closet, which I'd never looked in before. It was full of books that had been put there way back when. The table kept on spelling out 'monkeys in the closet,' so I started pulling books out. And there at the back of the closet, under all those books, was a carved ivory statue with twelve ivory monkeys on it. There was a tree, and the monkeys were going up the tree.

"We were all very sober by this time and getting quite nervous. It was about two in the morning. A friend who had gone out for dinner came back and said she smelled brimstone in the house. We said don't be silly.

"Finally, the table spelled out, 'Bury me in the garden.'

"One of the guests said we had to have a bell, book, and candle, so we found all that and took it out to the Chinese garden, across a big lawn. We dug a hole, buried the statue in it, and covered it up. Then we walked back to the big house.

"Bill Archibald went to his room, and came out and said, 'Come on . . .' On his pillow he had found one of the little monkeys. There was no way he could have taken it off the statue; they weren't detachable, it was all one carving, one piece of ivory.

"But the weekend's happenings weren't over. The next morning, when we were saying goodbye to our friends, we found another of these little ivory monkeys on the steps of the front door."

The famous psychic Eileen Garrett had been a consultant during the production of *The Innocents*, and Beatrice told her what had happened.

"She said go back and dig it up," Beatrice says. "She said don't do these things unless you're with somebody who really knows what it's all about, that there are spirits who are naughty and can cause trouble. So the next weekend my husband and I went back to the house, and we went to the garden and dug, and there was no statue."

15
THE SPIRIT OF LEE STRASBERG VISITS HIS GRANDDAUGHTER

The next two chapters concern the same family—that of the late Lee Strasberg, who might well be termed the leading teacher of acting in twentieth-century America. He was one of the founders and the artistic director of the Actors Studio in New York. The Studio was the stronghold of method acting, and was sometimes called, only partially facetiously, The Temple. Strasberg was certainly the high priest.

Among his students were many young actors who went on to fame. A partial listing includes Al Pacino, Robert DeNiro, Ellen Burstyn, Marlon Brando, Jane Fonda, Joanne Woodward, Anne Bancroft, Karl Malden, Sidney Poiter, Maureen Stapleton, Julie Harris, Paul Newman, Eli Wallach, Eva Marie Saint, and Geraldine Page.

Although Strasberg was best known as a director and teacher, he began as an actor and occasionally took roles throughout his life. He might be best known to a wide audience as one of the three elderly bank robbers, along with George Burns and Art Carney, in the film *Going in Style.*

Strasberg died in 1981 at the age of eighty. Since then a number of relatives and friends have reported contacts with him. For example, Burstyn is quoted as saying she had contact with Strasberg about twenty-four hours after his death. She was staying with his widow, Anna, in the Strasberg apartment.

"As I was trying to get to sleep," Burstyn has been quoted, "I suddenly felt a pull on my shoulder, and Lee appeared on my 'inner screen.' He said to me, 'Be strong. Don't let Anna or the children get the wrong idea about death. Yes, grieve, but death is part of life, and not the end.' "

Burstyn has a considerable interest in spirituality. She is a member of the Sufis, a spiritual group, and played a spiritual healer in the film *Resurrection.*

Strasberg has a daughter, Susan, who has gained substantial recognition in the theater and film world. When she was twenty, she played the title role in *The Diary of Anne Frank* on Broadway. She has lived in California for many years, has appeared in many films, and teaches acting. She is also very much involved in mysticism.

When I spoke to her, she was at first reluctant to speak of her experiences, since she was writing a book herself. "It's called *In My Father's House,*" she said, "and deals with my paranormal and spiritual odyssey." She said she has been involved with the metaphysical for about twenty-five years. "I've talked with some people more after they died than I did before they died," she laughed.

Susan Strasberg

Although Susan did not want to talk specifically about her own experiences with her father, she was quite willing to talk about those of her daughter, Jennie.

"My daughter used to see my mother when she was very young," Susan says. "They never met. My mother died the same month Jennie was born. When Jennie was about three years old she used to say, 'The lady with the long, red hair visited me again last night.' That is what my mother looked like. Jennie had never seen a picture of my mother in color. I believe it was my mother coming to take a look at her granddaughter.

"My father has come through Jennie, too. She's very sensitive and psychic. She had a number of experiences as a child. She didn't like it, though, which is just as well. My feeling is that you open those doors when you're ready to.

"A few years ago, Jennie was doing some hypnosis therapy. She wanted to work on weight and some problems. She was in a light hypnosis, working with a psychiatrist who's a hypnotherapist. Suddenly there was this whole long message from my father, a very specific message to go some place at a certain time and certain things would happen. This was taped. It was something that only my father would know. It was something that my father had to spell out for her because she couldn't even pronounce the word—what to look for.

"Afterward, Jennie said, 'This can't be real. I made it up. I'm crazy, Mother, they'll lock me up.' This was before Shirley MacLaine. Jennie used to think I was crazy; now she thinks I'm normal compared to her.

"So I called the psychiatrist, as well as a friend of mine, and we talked about it, and I said, 'Once you start playing this kind of game you've got to follow it through. Let's follow the message and see if it will be accurate or if it's nothing.' The night before we went to do this quest my father had sent us on, we were having a dinner party. Jennie was sitting at the table, with her eyes open, and she said, 'Grandpa's here, and he gave me this message. I wrote it all down.' The next day we went to do this thing and not only was the message clear, it was 90 percent accurate. The major thing we went to look for was there.

"My father, by the way, was not a believer. He was very wary of all this. Mysticism was a dirty word to him, I think partially because he didn't understand it. I think he was afraid of it.

"But someone sent me a videotape of a show he had been on shortly before he died, and he talks about his mother being around, that he could see her face. So even with his resistance, he had had a paranormal experience that had scared the hell out of him, the year before he died. I feel that it was all preparation."

16
THE WILD AND CRAZY LADY WHO HAUNTED SUSAN STRASBERG'S HOUSE

When Susan Strasberg moved to California to do film work, she and her then-husband, Christopher Jones, bought a house in Beverly Hills that had belonged to the well-known British character actor, Sir Cedric Hardwicke.

"This was in the sixties," Susan told me. "Christopher said he kept seeing this woman in the house, that he thought she lived in an upstairs room. Being an actor and a little eccentric, he used to talk to this lady and invite her to come dance with him. I would just get chills. I felt very strange about that upstairs room.

"Then I had a girlfriend who was a medical doctor who came and stayed there and said that in the middle of the night she woke up and there was someone pressing on her throat and chest, and that she had an impression of a woman, who then disappeared. I thought this was all imagination, that we were creating this.

123

We project outward, I think; some of the things we see are projections. Sometimes our fears become manifest and are projected outward. So you have to differentiate between what actually is separate and what is coming from the unconscious, especially if you're very powerful as a psychic.

"Then one day I got a call from a friend of mine in New York, and he said, 'I'm sitting here with Cedric Hardwicke's son and he wants to know how's the lady. I said, 'What lady?' And he said, 'The lady who haunts the upstairs room.' And I said, 'I wish you hadn't told me this.'

"More and more people who came to the house started becoming aware of this. They'd say, 'Isn't there somebody upstairs?' I started getting very nervous.

"At night, Christopher would say, 'She's here.' And I'd go under the covers and say, 'You tell her to stay on her side of reality and I'll stay on mine."

"I had candles burning, and Bibles, and Jewish stars, and Buddhas. I wasn't taking any chances.

"I had this girlfriend who had been my stand-in in Italy. She was a little girl, in her twenties, almost an albino, very fair. She was half Russian, half German. I worked with her on a film with Dirk Bogarde called *The High Bright Sun* [1965] that was shot in southern Italy. When this little girl and I walked down the street the people thought she was a witch, and they'd make a protective sign. They're very superstitious in Bari, that southern tip of Italy. There was something about her, maybe being almost an albino, that made them think she was psychic, which to them would be a witch. And she *was* very psychic.

"Her name was Marina DeYorzo. The only film I

can think of that she was in was that Fellini film "Toby Dammit," which is a segment of the 1968 omnibus film *Spirit of the Dead* with Terence Stamp, where he makes a bargain with the devil. There's a little, innocent girl who follows him around, bouncing a big ball. That was Marina."

This rang a bell with me, although I didn't remember the character as being so innocent. Years ago I saw that picture and had never forgotten this girl who bounced a ball around after the hero, gazing at him longingly. The hero, Terence Stamp, played an English actor on his last legs who was appearing in an Italian film. At the end of the picture, he commits suicide by driving his open sports car off a precipice. But a warning cable has been stretched across the brink of the precipice, and it neatly slices his head off, cutting his life even shorter by a few seconds. The young girl, a background character so far, now comes center screen. She drops her ball and runs to pick up the pretty blond head. That was why she'd been following him around throughout the film. The character had no lines— she just drifted in and out in the background— but it was an unforgettable bit part.

"Marina," Susan said, "came to spend a month in America and came to stay with me for a couple of weeks. During the course of her visit we were doing something like yoga breathing, something that altered consciousness. All of a sudden she started to say in that strange accent—German, like Marlene Dietrich—'Wiolet, I see wiolet. How beautiful. Oh, I love it!' And then she said, 'Oh, there's a woman.' And she started to describe this woman, this ghost. I said, 'That's enough. Let's just say a little prayer and invocation. . . .' And she said, 'Oh, she's coming toward me! She's trying to take over my body, she wants to possess me!'

"She was talking in this terrified voice. There were two men friends of my husband in the room, and I said, 'We've got to get her out of the house!' Well, she was so strong! She was about five feet one, a little, tiny, skinny girl. But she started fighting and resisting being taken out of the house, and we could not get her out. Finally, we managed to half-drag her into the backyard. Next door we had a very nice, low-key, sort of conservative neighbor, and I just hoped he wouldn't see this.

"I started calling people on the phone, asking what do we do? And they're saying, well, you have to do these prayers and make a circle around her, and so on. I'm saying the Lord's Prayer and I'm saying invocations. I'm sprinkling salt, I'm doing everything I've ever read about or heard of. I've got mediums on the phone, and a reverend who helped with things like this.

"Finally, we decided to get her out of the house by the front door so we could get her away from the place. We managed to drag and carry her through the house. She had the strength of ten men, she was moaning and going through convulsions. I just wanted to get her away from that house. It wasn't something I wanted going on in my house with a guest of mine.

"So finally we managed to get her out the front door. The men had scratches on their faces, and they were bruised, she was so strong. The minute we got her over the threshold, the second, she suddenly stopped moaning, stopped struggling, and she said, 'What's the matter? Put me down! Why are you holding me?'

"So when we told her, she wanted to go back into the house. She wasn't going to be intimidated. But I said,

'No we're not!' And we packed suitcases and went to a hotel till she left.

"In the meantime, I had people come in to clear the house, try to talk to this spirit and dehaunt the place. We had a priest come in, we had a metaphysician, we had an Indian person. But I don't believe the house ever got cleared.

"I don't know who the woman was."

17
SHE FELT
A GHOST—
AND IT HURT!

While I was writing this book, I went to New York to a one-day symposium being given by *Psychic Guide* magazine in the Town Hall Theater. Interesting speakers included Bill Tenuto, a medium prominent in Chapter 12 of this book; Russell Targ, a well-known California physicist and parapsychologist; and Uri Geller, who probably needs no introduction anywhere in the Western world, and possibly the Eastern as well.

Paul Zuromski, publisher of *Psychic Guide,* had urged me to come, saying that there would be many psychics there and some might have stories to tell of the rich and famous. I asked him to make an announcement to the effect I was sitting in the third row, left, eagerly awaiting some usable material. Five people approached me during the day, all with interesting accounts; three found their way into this book.

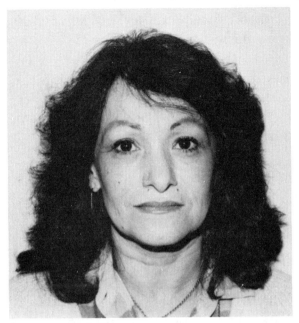

Joyce Caffey *(photo by Arthur Myers)*

One person who approached me at the conference was a small, attractive woman. She led off by saying she didn't have anything I would be interested in for the book, but she wanted to know if I had ever heard of the sort of thing that had happened to her. I had not, and although it did not involve a person known to readers in the United States, it did involve the first dancer of a ballet company in a South American country, who was an authentic celebrity in his own land. Because the woman's story was so fascinating and unusual, I am including it in this book.

Her name is Joyce Caffey, and she lives in Arlington, Texas. She told me she had been psychic from childhood. "I was very much aware of spirits," she says. "When I was young I had many, many spiritual playmates, whom I still remember. When I told my mother, she said, 'All kids do that.' " Caffey smiled ruefully and said, "Our world just takes it all away."

As a result of the disbelief and disapproval she encountered, Caffey turned away from her psychic ability. "I had very much fear of it," she says, "I would never acknowledge it. I would never let anything that was of the supernatural, including movies or books, near me."

One time, she says, she saw an apparition of her dead grandmother, and it frightened her so much she willed it to go away. She says, "I have willed my spirit vision to go away, but I hear spirits, smell them, sense them."

Caffey clung to the mundane life, getting married, having two sons, working for twenty-five years in the medical field. She became a business consultant for a group of surgeons. Then four years ago, as a result of a near-death experience triggered by an adverse reaction to an antibiotic, her life changed.

She says her consciousness expanded and her values changed. "I became much more in touch with my own spirituality." She quit her job. "I didn't want to be around people anymore who didn't like themselves or each other, whom you couldn't please no matter what. The near-death experience opened the door to my acknowledgment of there being more to reality than what was right in front of my eyes, which I had been bound and determined would be the only thing I would see."

She says she found she had a new energy, which she didn't understand, that seemed to help people and organizations to work and expand. Through a mutual friend, she met, on the phone, a woman in New York whom we will call Marie. "All of a sudden," Joyce says,

"I knew there was something I had to do for this lady."

Marie is a linguist—a translator and teacher. While in Paris, she met her future husband, a South American dancer; they are now divorced. He had been a student of a famed dancer and choreographer whom we will call Roberto. "Roberto," Marie told me, "had a reputation for being a very noble and generous person, very helpful to people."

Marie and Roberto became friends. They organized an arts association to promote South American folk art in the United States. Dancers were imported and concerts were scheduled at a number of U.S. universities.

Roberto, however, was stricken with cancer and had become bedridden. In March 1987, the association was to hold its premier performance at a university near New York City. Marie asked Joyce to come up from Texas to "lend a helping hand."

The moment Joyce got off the airplane in New York and met Marie, she was filled with physical pain. "The pains were excruciating," she says, "on the left side of my abdominal area and radiating up through my chest."

They went to Marie's apartment, and Joyce found herself possessed of an overwhelming urge for a cigarette. "I quit smoking over a year ago," she says, "but the minute I walked into that apartment I had to have a cigarette. I told Marie I had this incredible urge, and she pointed to a cigarette but it didn't taste good to me. But the craving was so intense. I kept saying, this is the most ridiculous thing, why do I want this cigarette?

"I found myself so impressed with Marie," Joyce says. "I had thoughts about how wonderful she was. I didn't understand it, my looking at her and being so impressed. She wasn't doing anything yet that was so spectacular, in my awareness."

The powerful pains continued during the next two days.

Two days after Joyce's arrival, they went to the university auditorium for the debut dance performance of the association. "I was incredibly cold," Joyce recalls. "I kept going to get coffee because I was so cold. But the people around me weren't cold. The only other time I have been so cold is when my husband died, right after his funeral, and I knew he was in the room with me."

That Sunday night Marie called a woman in South America to find out how Roberto was and to ask her to tell him the performance had been successful. She was told he had died two days before.

Joyce's pains immediately stopped. They had been in the same bodily area where Roberto had been affected.

Joyce says she is puzzled by the experience, but she is not really at a loss as to what had happened. "I didn't want to let Marie think that Roberto's spirit had entered me," she says, "but I have a way of discerning spirits now. This is a part of me."

I have a personal addendum to this account. I interviewed Marie on the phone for a half hour. During the last few minutes of the conversation her voice got fainter and fainter, so much so that by the time we hung up I could barely hear her. If we had not been finished with the interview, I would have suggested that I call back to get a better connection. A more startling surprise was in store for me. I had taped the interview, and the next day when I played it back I found that although my voice was strong throughout, in many places Marie's voice was nonexistent.

As I replayed the tape, I found that during the first ten minutes or so her voice was clear. Then, as I began to ask questions about Roberto, her replies became less discernible. Her voice was often interrupted on the tape, leaving gaps between words or for whole sentences. Before long, there was only silence between my questions; her voice was not on the tape at all.

About ten minutes before the end of the tape, our conversation became more general. I had recently been in Mexico, and I mentioned a performance of the Mexican Folclórico company I had seen in Mexico City. We talked about her plans for the association. During this part of the conversation, her voice came back on the tape, at normal volume.

But when the conversation turned again to Roberto, her voice on the tape blanked out again. It did not come back on.

III

THE
POLITICAL
SCENE

18
JIMMY AND ROSALYNN CARTER'S HAUNTED HOUSE

When Jimmy and Rosalynn Carter were a young couple, they lived in Plains, Georgia, in a house that local tradition insisted was haunted. They had at least one experience that seemed to indicate the neighborhood lore might have held some truth.

Jimmy had left the navy and returned to Plains to help run the family peanut business. In 1956 they moved into the old house with their three sons and stayed there until 1960, when they moved into a house they built.

The old house, dating from 1850, was set in a grove of tall magnolia trees. It had a wide center hall, many fireplaces, and two front rooms, one on the east side of the hall, the other on the west side. The rooms had old, hand-planed floorboards running their eighteen-foot widths. The west room was particularly suspect as the haven of a ghost.

Jimmy and Rosalynn Carter

Rosalynn's memories of the house go back to her childhood. "When I was a little girl," she said in the May 1979 issue of *Good Housekeeping* "my best friend was Jimmy's sister Ruth [Ruth Carter Stapleton]. We had to pass the 'haunted house' to visit each other. We were about eleven and so afraid of the house that we took the long way around."

"I wasn't really afraid of the ghost when we moved in," Rosalynn said. But she never went into that front room at night after The Incident: "Our living room furniture was in this room," she said, "but there was no heat so we didn't use it very often. One night we heard a crash in there. We waited a bit, and then the whole family trooped in together, thinking a window had fallen shut. But the window was still wide open. So I wasn't afraid of living in the house, but I would not have gone into that room at night by myself."

Inez Laster, who worked as a cook in the house just before the Carters moved in, reported some interesting experiences. "Things would happen in that front room," she said. "I could hear knocking on the door. Then it would open and shut and I'd hear walking. I'd see a woman with a long, white dress."

Her employer, Dr. Thaddeus Wise, could see the apparition too, according to Laster. "He'd say it was our imagination, but when he spoke to the woman she and the light she carried both vanished. Sometimes I'd hear her walking on the attic stairs."

Like many supposedly haunted houses, this one had a history of a quick turnover of occupants. One tenant told of having the sheets snatched off the bed in the middle of the night. Another item in the oral history of the house is a small white dog who is seen coming up onto the front porch and who promptly disappears if anyone reaches down to pat it.

A dozen years after moving out of the house, while Jimmy was governor of Georgia, Rosalynn and some friends, in an antic mood, decided to tour the house to see if they could discover why the place would be haunted. They were already aware of a secret compartment tucked between the floor of the attic and just over the "haunted" front room. The Carter boys had discovered the little room when they were playing in the attic and noticed a loose brick in a fireplace. They found the bricks and the boards under them would lift out to allow access to the small room.

The reason for a hidden room has been lost in the mists of time. Was it a hiding place for the Underground Railroad, or for Confederate soldiers? Could it have been a refuge for escaped prisoners from nearby Andersonville Prison?

During the group's ghost-hunting expedition in 1973, a small boy in the party discovered another concealed room by prying up bricks from a fireplace on the other side of the attic.

So that makes two hidden rooms, at least, in this old house. But who the ghost is and why it is there is still a mystery.

19
DID MAMIE EISENHOWER'S GHOST HEAD OFF A PARKING LOT IN HER BACKYARD?

In 1950, when Dwight Eisenhower was president of Columbia University, he and his wife, Mamie, looked for a country retreat. They bought a run-down farmhouse adjacent to the Gettysburg battlefield in Pennsylvania and restored it. When Ike became president of the United States in 1952, he had use of Camp David, the official presidential retreat, but the Eisenhowers often preferred their Gettsyburg farmhouse.

When Ike left the White House in 1960, he and Mamie went immediately to the Gettysburg house, their home base. Ike died in 1969; Mamie continued living at the farmhouse until her death in 1979. The farmhouse then became a national historical site, administered by the National Park Service of the U.S. Department of the Interior. It is open to the public.

Within the past few years, strange things have happened at the house.

Priscilla Baker, special assistant to the director of the National Park Service, has an interest in psychic phenomena, so the staff of the Eisenhower farmhouse approached her. In 1982, she brought in a highly respected Washington psychic, Anne Gehman. Gehman has been a consultant to a number of federal agencies and to some of the country's best-known corporations, has worked with police in many states, and has been the object of research by major universities.

"Anne went to the Eisenhower farm at my request," Baker told me. "The rangers assigned to that park area were seeing and hearing a great many very peculiar things. Two rangers in particular were very, very upset and wanted to leave. They wanted to quit the Park Service altogether."

Lights were flicking on and off in the front hall, and electricians could find no cause. The rangers heard music coming from an empty guest room. Rangers on duty at night heard, sometimes saw, doors open and slam shut. They heard thumping noises. "That's the kind of thing that made the rangers terribly, terribly nervous," Baker told me.

One of the rangers continually saw an apparition of Mamie. As Baker puts it: "This ranger had no grounding in matters psychical. She had no background, had done no reading, had heard no lectures, didn't know a thing about it. All she knew was that every now and then she'd walk into the living room of the house, and in the far corner of the room she would see Mrs. Eisenhower. She thought she was ready for the local laughing academy.

"Anne explained to her that she was not ready for the local laughing academy, that Mrs. Eisenhower's spirit

•

was very much in evidence, that she was often in the living room, and also that she often spent time in the bedroom looking out the window.

"The president's presence was not as strong. Anne did not communicate with the president particularly except to acknowledge his presence. He was in his study, which is on the first floor, by the back entrance. It looks like a library, with bookshelves. He spent most of his time there."

According to Baker, Gehman also was aware of Mrs. Eisenhower's mother—Mrs. Dowd—and a military aide of the president.

One spirit with whom Gehman had definite communication was Rose Wood, Mrs. Eisenhower's maid. It was Wood, Gehman said, who was flicking the lights on and off.

According to Baker, "Rose told Anne that she wanted everybody to know she had never been happier in her life on earth than when she was working for Mrs. Eisenhower. She said she planned to stay in the house, and she had been working the lights just to let people know she was there. And now that Anne had conveyed that message she wouldn't work the lights anymore. And they haven't gone on and off since."

During her visit to the farmhouse Gehman picked up a number of other spirits, including that of a little boy about eight or ten. She could not identify the boy, but felt he had some sort of relationship with the Eisenhower family. She said she also kept picking up a spirit whose name sounded like Clinton.

Baker says, "The name wasn't clear; it wasn't Clinton but it sounded like Clinton. The park historian didn't know who she was talking about, but he went rooting through his records and came up with a note about a man named Quentin Armstrong, the first white settler in that area, who had built a farmhouse on the property the Eisenhowers purchased.

"A portion of the foundation of the house was built around a large boulder," Baker says. "Anne communicated with Indian spirits who indicated to her that the clearing on which the house originally had been built had been of considerable religious significance before the white settlers had arrived. The boulder had been a focal point for the Indians' religious observances. She was told by an Indian spirit that the Park Service should devote more attention to the Indian history of the area, that there was an important lesson to be learned there. And as a matter of fact, the Park Service has now done that.

"There is a garden behind the house. In the center of this area there is an old well that dates from the Civil War era. Anne went into the garden and said there were human remains buried beside the well. She said if you dig down there you'll find human remains. The members of the park staff who were in attendance had known nothing of that at all, but they were not inclined to dig up the garden. A year or two later, one of the park's staff was recording an oral history with a gardener who had worked for the Eisenhowers. The gardener said he had come across evidence of human remains and had asked Mrs. Eisenhower what to do about it. She said no one knows who it is, so rebury them and let them rest in peace."

Gehman told me, "Mamie was concerned that they were going to tear up part of the yard for a parking lot and she was very opposed to that. That was one of the communications that came through. I don't know what influence this communication had, but they didn't go ahead with it after that."

Gehman says she communicated with the president but did not recall details. There was some discussion of the Eisenhowers' children, she said, and of some things that were going on at the farm. I asked if she thought these apparitions and communications could be place memories—energy imprinted on a space that is thought to account for some psychic manifestations. "No," she said, "these were definitely the real spirits of these people."

I asked if these might be earthbound spirits, people who clung to the physical world, refusing to move on to higher planes. "No," she replied, "I don't think they're just hanging around. I think there's a tremendous effort on the part of the spirit world many times to work through sensitive individuals. I don't think that when a person passes on they necessarily just leave everything behind. I think their interest still remains with those things and people and those situations that they've loved and cared for. I don't think that it's that they're just hanging around; they're just there part of the time. It was their home and they still have an interest in it."

20
MACKENZIE KING, CANADA'S FAMED PRIME MINISTER—OR, HOW TO RUN A COUNTRY AND STILL HAVE TIME FOR THE NEXT WORLD

William Lyon Mackenzie King was prime minister of Canada from 1921 to 1930, and from 1935 to 1948, longer than any other prime minister in the history of the British Commonwealth. He was a short, squat, seemingly ultraconventional man of Scots-Canadian background. He was a very successful politician and a brilliant statesman if you were of the liberal—upper-case or lower-case—persuasion and merely a clever pol if you were conservatively inclined. Although world famous, he was no Roosevelt or Churchill. If the term *charismatic* had been in such fervent use in his day as it is now, it never would have been applied to him. A dour Scot, a devout Presbyterian, and a lifelong bachelor; apparently no other woman could displace his mother, even after her death.

King's conservative image was turned upside down in 1951, a year after he had died at age seventy-six. King was revealed as an enthusiastic participant in séances,

Mackenzie King

a constant communicator with his deceased mother, brother, sister, Franklin Delano Roosevelt, his dog Pat, and various others. He also was disclosed as a secret womanizer, usually of the pay-to-play variety. It gave Canadians quite a bit to talk about for a while.

In the summer of 1987, a four-hour documentary on King's life was being prepared by the Canadian Broadcasting Corporation. Its author and director was Don Brittain, who had once been a cub reporter on the Ottawa *Journal*. In an interview in the Toronto *Globe and Mail*, Brittain told reporter Mike Boone that he

*The crystal ball King acquired in London and a statuette of his
beloved dog, Pat*   *(photo by Arthur Myers)*

remembered King as "essentially an embarrassment—
boring, long-winded, and ugly. The only people we
wanted to see were Roosevelt and Churchill. When we
saw the great war leaders, we hoped King wouldn't
show up and embarrass us."

But when King's other side was posthumously revealed, Brittain says, "It was a great shock to those of
us who grew up with King as this dowdy, pot-bellied,
sanctimonious prig. It gave him another dimension."

Reporter Boone put it this way: "In the minds of
Canadians, King somehow went from dullard to
wacko without touching second base."

In researching this chapter, I had an advantage in
that a friend of mine is a cousin of A. Edgar Ritchie,
who has held important posts in the Canadian government. He was at one time the Canadian ambassador to
the United States. Through him I was able to meet a

The main house on King's country estate *(photo by Arthur Myers)*

number of people who had had close contact with Mackenzie King. One of these was Jack Pickersgill, who in his youth had been an aide to King, and who had himself gone on to hold important positions in the government. Pickersgill told me: "He was awfully naive in some ways, Mackenzie King. He thought an awful lot of things were secret that in fact weren't. In those days the press didn't publish a lot of things about people's private lives. If they had, he might have had as hard a time as Gary Hart."

King's interest in the occult . . . the psychic . . . the spiritual . . . however it might be termed, became widely known in December 1951, somewhat over a year after his death, when *Maclean's*, Canada's leading magazine, published an article titled "The Secret Life of Mackenzie King, Spiritualist," by Blair Fraser, a well-known *Maclean's* staffer. In an extensive article, Fraser wrote:

"Mr. King was not a member of the Spiritualist Church and spiritualism was not a religion to him; he remained to the end of his days a good Presbyterian. But he did believe in the life after death, not as a matter of faith but as a proven fact."

Although Fraser scooped his colleagues of the general press, the story had already been known in certain circles. In his article he reported that King had not been dead a fortnight before a statement to the effect that King had been conducting the affairs of Canada on advice from the spirit world was published in the spiritualist weekly *Psychic News*.

Fraser took pains to avoid that implication, however, saying King sought contact with his dead relatives and friends not to consult them on affairs of state but simply to talk with them. This caveat pops up throughout the King psychic literature, and well it might, since he was numbering among his other-worldly communicators such notables as FDR, Queen Victoria, and Sir Wilfred Laurier. (Laurier is considered Canada's most eminent prime minister; he was a predecessor of King's and was King's idol in his younger days.) In fact there seems almost an overabundance of protest on this point. Particularly in view of the fact that about three years before his death, King's mother supposedly warned him from her vantage point in the next world to retire, that his heart could not stand the pace at which he was driving himself. Franklin Roosevelt, however, had a different opinion. He is reputed to have said to King through a medium, "Don't retire, stay on the job. Your country needs you there."

This séance was held in England, and afterward the medium got another message from FDR to the effect that he had changed his mind, that he now thought King's health too precarious for him to continue in office. The medium passed the word along to King in Ottawa.

However, the medium, Geraldine Cummins, was quoted as sayng that King made it a rule to ignore advice volunteered at sittings; he trusted solely to his own and his advisers' judgment."

It is believed that one of the first mediums that King made a habit of consulting was Etta Wriedt of Detroit. Internationally known, she made many visits to Great Britain and held séances for famous people. King first met her in the 1920s, or possibly the early 1930s. His mother had died in 1917, and he was loathe to relinquish the close relationship he had had with her. King was highly impressed with Wriedt when the widow of a friend of his, a Canadian senator, asked Wriedt to locate her husband's lost will. Wriedt told her the missing document would be found in a certain house in France, and it was. This greatly impressed King, a very practical man. The late Nandor Fodor, a psychoanalyst and psychic researcher, wrote that King "as a result of years of personal inquiries, came to accept human survival after death as a demonstrable fact, but never ceased to be critical in appraising the evidence."

Nevertheless, it would hardly be politic for a politician in our mundane world to have it bruited about that he thought he was tapping into another dimension. This could well be a one-way ticket to obscurity. And so Mackenzie King tried to keep it under his hat. I spoke with his personal secretary, J.E. Handy, who obviously took a dim view of the whole affair, but was

Laurier House in Ottawa, where King lived when he was prime minister   (photo by Arthur Myers)

loyal to his longtime employer. "He did *not* believe in ghosts," Handy said. "He was interested in psychical research. It was a quest for the unknown; that doesn't mean ghosts, oh, no! We went to some séances in London at the Queensbury Club; that's a place where people tried to communicate with the souls of the departed. It was more of a hobby than anything else with him. The reason we never spoke out about it was because it was just a sport, a hobby. I was present at one of these séances and I can vouch for the fact that it had nothing to do with his political life. I think it has been grossly exaggerated."

A crystal ball is on display at Laurier House, where King lived when he was prime minister, and Handy told a story of how King acquired it. "We were in London and he was buying souvenirs, and there was an expensive crystal ball. It was something like seven hundred dollars. He said that's too much. We walked back to our hotel and the first thing you know it was presented to him with a card from an American admirer who had recognized him in the shop."

I asked if King had ever used the ball.

"No, he didn't," Handy replied.

One time in London, King was short of cash to attend a séance or some other psychic event. He asked Hardy to borrow fifty pounds from Jack Pickersgill but not tell him what it was for. Pickersgill was not sympathetic to psychic inquiries. In fact, when I first spoke with him by phone, his opening words were, "I should warn you, I don't believe in spooks."

When I later spoke to Pickersgill in person, I mentioned what Handy had told me. "I knew what I was loaning King the fifty pounds for," Pickersgill said, smiling. "He knew I would never tell." And he went on to comment that King's associates knew a lot more about him than he knew they knew.

Although it might seem that King's predilection for the occult was a slightly open secret some time before his death, Blair Fraser was the first journalist to really spill the beans. Handy told me that he had given Fraser some help on the story.

"I'm the one who gave him the names of those spiritualists in London," he said. "There were rumors around Ottawa. He invited me to go to lunch with him one day and I liked him very much, so I gave him a good lead on it."

Fraser showed Handy the article before it was published. Handy greatly objected to Fraser's mention of the dog Pat. "I said, 'Look, Fraser, we know that a dog has not got an immortal soul. Once a dog is dead, he's dead.' But he left it in the article, so that was the end of my connection with him. There's no use going for trash like that."

Much of the King legend is based on King's diaries, which he dictated to Handy. "Those diaries are something like Nixon's tapes," Handy told me. "I sometimes feel those diaries should have been destroyed."

The author-director of the CBC documentary, Don Brittain, relied heavily on the diaries. Handy said, "The actor who is portraying me was here to see me a couple of weeks ago to see if I was still with this world. I straightened him out on a few things."

But the leaks about King's interest in the occult should not be overemphasized. For example, the book considered the most authoritative biography of King is *The Incredible Canadian*, by Bruce Hutchison, a highly regarded journalist and author, and he told me: "I wrote a long book about Mackenzie King, but I did not know and nobody knew at the time this book was published [in 1952] that King was a spiritualist. That story didn't break till some time after his death. I saw a great deal of King, and he was very candid with me about everythng, but never discussed that with anybody."

I told Hutchison that I had seen an article written by journalist Percy J. Philip, in which Philip claimed not only to have seen King's ghost but to have carried on a discussion with it.

"Well," Hutchison commented, "I know a great deal about King's public life in this world but nothing about his adventures in the next. But I've no objection to it, as my good friend Jack Pickersgill has. Jack and I don't agree on this sort of thing. King was very religious in another sense. He was a great fellow for reading the Bible every morning, he kept his cabinets waiting while he was dealing with prayer. He was a great Presbyterian and went to church at all times."

In more recent years, a book with a highly sensational impact has been published. The author is C.P. Stacey; the title is *A Very Double Life*; the subtitle is *The Private World of Mackenzie King*. The book is not friendly toward King; it is, in fact, quite hostile. King's outré sex life and spiritual life are dealt with in some detail. In fact, while in Ottawa consorting mostly with liberals, I constantly heard the book referred to as "scurrilous." I did, however, meet one quasimilitary type who thought it was a pretty good book, and thereby hangs a tale.

During World War II, King refused to allow conscription. His rationale was that it would tear the country apart. This did not set at all well with military people. Stacey, a respected scholar, was the official Canadian Army historian. He was not about to let King down easily. He begins one chapter:

"At the beginning of 1898 Mackenzie King . . . aged twenty-three, was in serious trouble. He was tormented by the sexual urges that drove him to associate with prostitutes, and by the religious beliefs that told him that associating with prostitutes was a sin. He himself frequently said that he came to the brink of insanity; and those who read his diary will be inclined to agree."

Most of the people I talked with in Ottawa protested that Stacey had taken scenes from King's callow youth and made it sound as though he were chasing hookers up and down the streets of Ottawa until a ripe old age. That isn't cricket, I thought, and decided to ignore the book. After all, we're talking about the other world here, not something as earthly as sex. Although it certainly would liven up the chapter. Then I had a chat with Don Brittain, the TV man.

"The best guy on the subject of King is Stacey," he said. "His book is very accurate. I checked King's diaries, and it's there. Everything that Stacey said is taken from the diaries."

I mentioned my liberal friends' accusations that Stacey had distorted King's youthful indiscretions.

"Well," Brittain said, "the last reference to it in the diaries that I saw was in 1917. At that point he was forty-three or thereabouts. I just talked to Walter Turnbull, who was a secretary to King, and he told me, 'I believe this stuff. There were some rather dubious looking ladies you'd see at Laurier House.' King refers to 'the dark urges' in his diaries in 1939, that were still there. He'd write, 'I wasted another night. Can I never calm the fire of my body and subdue it to the glory of the soul? And it cost me a dollar fifty.' So there's no question what he is talking about.

"Stacey obviously harbored a dislike of King for a long time, and in a sense he was out to get him, but the book is very sound, everything that he said is from the diaries. The stuff is there, and some of it is very wild stuff."

Stacey did not treat King's interest in the occult in a sympathetic tone, to say the least. In one passage, he speaks of a trip King took to the United States:

"It did not . . . occur to King that it might be politic

for the prime minister of Canada to curb his spiritualistic activities when in a foreign country. In December
1935 . . . he spent a day in New York and had a long
sitting with a medium. Then, hearing that there were
good teacup readings at a tearoom on Fifth Avenue
called 'The Gypsy Tent,' he went there for another long
session."

But not all writers were unsympathetic, or even skeptical, about King's psychic activities. One well-known
member of the Ottawa press corps, Percy Philip, wrote
articles and went on the CBC stating that in 1954 he
had encountered the ghost of King and had had an
extended conversation with him. Philip's journalistic
credentials were impeccable; he had covered the Canadian government for the *New York Times* for some
twenty-five years.

I called the *Times* foreign desk to try to find out
something about Philip, but no one on duty that day
had ever heard of him; after all, he dated back at least
thirty years. But Victor Mackie, who had been chief of
bureau in Ottawa for a group of newspapers, remembers Philip well.

"He was very dignified," Mackie told me, "very self-
conscious about working for the *New York Times*. He
let you know as soon you met him that he worked for
the *Times*. But he had a humorous glint in his eye.
When he did this story we in the press gallery thought
he was pulling our legs. We asked him what he had
been drinking lately and he just passed it off. We in the
gallery all treated it as a Philip pull-your-leg sort of
thing. I don't know to this day whether he really saw a
specter of King or whether he just dreamed it up as a
joke on a dull day."

According to Nandor Fodor, in his book *They Knew the Unknown*, Philip published his account in *Liberty* magazine in January 1955. I saw a similar article by Philip in the *Fate* magazine of October 1955. I called Curtis Fuller, the editor and publisher, and he remembered the article.

"It was not a reprint," Fuller told me, "he wrote it for us." I told Fuller that I had heard in Ottawa that Philip's story about King's ghost was suspected of being a put-on. There was an almost audible gulp over the phone, although somewhat muted by the passage of thirty-two years. "That's a possibility, I suppose," Fuller said. "The fact is, it could be. I don't know."

Philip began his *Fate* article as follows:

"On a June evening in 1954 I had a long conversation with the former Canadian prime minister William L. Mackenzie King as we sat on a bench in the grounds of his old summer home at Kingsmere, twelve miles from Ottawa. It seemed to me an entirely normal thing although I knew perfectly well that Mr. King had been dead for four years."

According to Philip, he had known of King's psychic inclinations for a long time, and in fact had discussed such matters with him.

"Having an open mind about the occult and being inquisitive by nature," Philip wrote in *Fate*, "I . . . managed to turn several conversations with Mr. King to this subject [while he was alive]. Once, especially, when we were crossing the Atlantic to Europe, he talked freely about his beliefs and experiences as we walked the deck.

" 'If one believes in God and a life after death,' he said, 'it is inevitable that one must believe that the spirits of those who have gone take an interest in the people and places they loved during their lives on earth. It is the matter of communication that is difficult. For myself I have found that the method of solitary, direct communion is best. After my father and mother died I felt terribly alone. But I also felt that they were near me. Almost accidentally I established contact by talking to them as if they were present and soon I began to get replies."

Philip told of sitting on a bench close to King's country house. He wrote, "I suppose I was in a receptive mood. . . . I became conscious that I was not alone. Someone sat on the park bench beside me. . . . Without turning my head, for somehow I feared to look, I said as naturally as I could, 'Good evening, Mr. King.'

"In that warm tone which always marked his conversation the voice of Mr. King replied, 'Good evening, Philip. I am so glad you spoke to me. . . . One of the rules which govern our conduct on this side is that we are like the children and must not speak unless we are spoken to. I suppose it is a good rule because it would be very disturbing if we went around talking to people. The sad thing is that so few of them ever talk to us.' "

Philip quoted King as saying, "I have heard things about my character, motives, political actions and even my personal appearance and habits that have made me laugh so loudly I thought I must break the sound barrier. And I have heard things about myself, too, that have made me shrink. . . . There are things that I said and did that I could regret, but, on this side, we soon learn to have no regrets. Life would be meaningless if we did not all make mistakes, and eternity intolerable if we spent it regretting them."

Philip said he then attempted to interview King. "I asked several [questions] but he answered with the same skill as marked his replies to questions in the House of Commons and at meetings with the press, divulging nothing. It was I who was interviewed. He was eager for news and it surprised me then, as it does now, that he seemed not to know fully what was happening in the world. The dead, I discovered, are not omniscient. Or perhaps what we think important is not important to them."

They spoke of Canadian domestic affairs, and of international developments. This is hardly what most people would talk about if they met a communicative ghost; they'd probably be more interested in how things were over there; they know how they are here. But King was a politician and Philip a *New York Times* reporter, so perhaps that explains it.

King spoke to Philip of his reason for returning to his country home. "I suppose I spend a good deal of time here. There is so much beauty and peace. It is good to have some familiar, well-loved place to spend time in, until one gets used to eternity."

Philip concluded his article as follows:

"We both rose from the bench—or at least I did. When I looked at him, as I then did for the first time directly, he seemed just as I had known him in life, just as when I had talked with him once at this very spot.

" 'I think you told me once that you are Scottish born and a wee bit 'fey,' " he said. 'It's a good thing to be. We have two worlds. Those people who think their world is the only one, and who take it and themselves too seriously, have a very dull time. Do come back and talk with me again.'

"I muttered words of thanks and then, following the habit of a lifetime, stretched out my hand to bid goodbye. He was not there."

A spoof? Possibly, but a passage from Fodor's book has a ring of earnest sincerity. Concluding a chapter on King, Fodor wrote:

"The reporter [Philip] explained the event in *Liberty* magazine, noting that 'in Scotland, where I was born, we believe in ghosts' and that an apparition of his grandfather had visited him when he was three years old. The impression had been vivid: he remembered the old man as 'wrapped in homespun plaid' and speaking with a slight Aberdeenshire accent. Yes, Philip wrote, he had spoken with King's ghost on that bench in June 1954, although 'what the explanation may be of such phenomena, I do not claim to understand.' He added: 'They may be due to psychic influence, to a stimulated imagination, or to that subconscious working of the mind which happens in dreams. Yet there is no incompatibility between being a Christian and a churchgoer, as Mr. King was, and being a searcher into the mystery of the hereafter.' "

21
DOES LINCOLN'S GHOST HAUNT THE WHITE HOUSE? QUEEN WILHELMINA, WINSTON CHURCHILL, AND RONALD REAGAN'S DOG REX HAVE THOUGHT SO

A book of this sort could hardly be taken seriously without a chapter devoted to Abe Lincoln. According to reports, Lincoln was very much involved in the spirit world during his life, and since his death, he has often been sensed, even seen, in the White House, sometimes by famous people.

When it comes to witnesses, the riches are embarrassing—one hardly knows where to start. Queen Wilhelmina of the Netherlands? Winston Churchill? Maureen Reagan?

There are those who would consider the last named the most fun member of her family, although her ballet dancer–journalist brother could be considered a close second. Maureen was named cochairperson of the Republican Party in spite of the unmistakable signs she's shown of being a dedicated eccentric. She came out in favor of the equal rights amendment, for one thing—quite eccentric for her father's set—and she's been known to travel with a stuffed animal—eccentric for any set. In addition, she is married to a man who is six feet, seven inches tall, but that could happen to any woman.

Her husband, Dennis Revell, needs a long bed. Apparently, when the couple visits the White House they sleep in the longest bed in the place, in the Lincoln Bedroom. Early in 1987, *Newsweek* quoted Maureen as saying, "I'm not kidding, we've really seen it." Meaning Lincoln's ghost.

What they seem to see is a sometimes red, sometimes orange, aura, but that was good enough for them, and it's good enough for me. The older Reagans are a bit more conservative. Nancy comes down firmly on the safe side. *Newsweek* quoted Nancy as stating, "If Ronnie is away for a night or something, I can be here alone. I'm not afraid. I don't hear Abe Lincoln knocking on my door."

A brave woman—or perhaps she's just not into the spirit of the thing. Ronnie is more of a sport about it. On Lincoln's birthday in 1987, he found himself involved in a talk and photo opportunity with a group of junior high school students and was quoted in the *New York Times* as follows:

"There's a legend in the White House that Lincoln is still there. As a matter of fact, people who have worked there through several presidents will go out of their way to tell you, yes, that they believe he is. Now I haven't seen him myself, but I have to tell you, I am puzzled, because every once in a while our little dog, Rex, will start down that long hall toward that room, just glaring as if he's seeing something, and barking, and he stops in front of Lincoln's door, the bedroom door. And once, early on in this, I just couldn't understand it, so I went down and I opened the door and I stepped in and I turned around for him to come on, and he stood there, barking and growling, and then started backing away—and would not go in the room. So the funny thing, though, is that I feel, unlike you might think about other ghosts, if he is still there, I don't have any fear at all. I think it would be wonderful to have a little meeting with him, and probably very helpful."

Now if that isn't great communication, I don't know what is.

It's a writers' axiom that the three most salable subjects to write about are Lincoln, doctors, and dogs. In fact, writers have been known to send articles titled "Lincoln's Doctor's Dog" off to the *Reader's Digest* and other high-paying publications—to no avail, in my case. But I always like to get a few dogs into my books. In this one, for example, there is Lady Brindle, the dog at the Flagler Museum in Florida who sometimes turns right and goes down the hall to greet some unseen presence instead of going left into her mistress's bedroom as she usually does. (See Chapter 27.)

I worked several dogs into my last book, *The Ghostly Register*. Not to mention a cat and a rat, but that's a couple of other stories. To stick with dogs, three of them in a back-country hotel in Alaska wouldn't go upstairs at all; they didn't like *any* of the second floor rooms. I was once interviewed by Noah Adams on the Public Broadcasting System's program, "All Things Considered," and he commented, "The dogs always know." I heartily concurred.

Aside from dogs, Lincoln's ghost in the White House has always seemed a lot more fun to me than to the great majority of the people who have lived there. But sometimes one can misjudge these public figures. Calvin Coolidge has never been considered a barrel of laughs, but I have an actor friend in Boston, Jim Cooke, who has been doing a one-man show as Silent Cal. In his laconic, New England style, it turns out that Cal could be a very funny man when he wanted to be; Jim was practically doing a stand-up comic routine during a sizeable portion of his show. I had dinner with Jim one night and mentioned I had heard that Grace Coolidge has been quoted as saying she saw Lincoln's ghost. Jim urged me to call the Coolidges' son, John, who lived in Connecticut, to check out the story.

John reacted not only with denial but with some indignation when I asked him about his mother's experience. Nothing like that ever happened, he exclaimed. However, the idea has definitely seen the light of print before. In his 1987 book, *Ghosts: Washington's Most Famous Ghost Stories*, John Alexander wrote:

"Grace Coolidge is said to have seen the specter of the president, too. In a newspaper account I read, she said that he was dressed 'in black, with a stole draped across his shoulders to ward off the drafts and chills of Washington's night air.' "

Well, if it was in a newspaper, it must be true.

Other first ladies have been quoted as saying they were aware of the presence of Lincoln in one way or another. *Washington Post* writer Jacqueline Lawrence reported that Eleanor Roosevelt's servant, Mary Evan, told of seeing Lincoln on the bed in his old room, pulling on his boots. "Other servants," Lawrence wrote, "said they had seen him lying quietly in his bed, and still others vowed that he periodically stood in the oval window of the main entrance of the White House. Mrs. Roosevelt herself never saw Lincoln, but she did admit that when working late she frequently felt a ghostly sort of presence."

Both Lady Bird Johnson and Jacqueline Kennedy Onassis are also reported to have been aware of the presence of Lincoln.

It is said that Winston Churchill, a person of some psychic sensitivity, saw Lincoln's ghost and refused to enter Lincoln's bedroom.

When Queen Wilhelmina of the Netherlands visited the White House during World War II, she related a psychic experience she had there to Franklin Roosevelt and other people at cocktails the next evening. She said she had heard a knock on the door of the Rose Room, where she was staying, late at night. She opened the door, and standing before her, his large frame taking up most of the doorway, was Abraham Lincoln. She said she fainted, and when she came to was lying on the floor.

Harry Truman is said to have been awakened one night by two distinct knocks on the door of his bedroom. He opened the door, but there was no one there, just a cold spot that went away as footsteps trailed off down the corridor. Lynda Johnson has told of a similar experience: a knocking at her door and no one outside.

Priscilla Baker, assistant to the director of the National Park Service, has done a paper on Lincoln sightings, and told me, "Lincoln's spirit has been seen walking up and down the second floor hall of the White House, knocking on doors. Various members of former first families have confirmed these sightings, and Secret Service guys have been said to say they have seen the spirit in the second floor hall.''

There seems little doubt that Lincoln was very much involved in what was then called spiritualism, although his law partner, William H. Herndon, called it superstition. In the volume *The Hidden Lincoln*, edited by Emanuel Hertz, Herndon is quoted as follows:

"That Mr. Lincoln was somewhat superstitious there can be no doubt. When Lincoln went down to New Orleans in '31 he consulted a fortune teller, asking her to give him his history, his end and his fate. She told him what it was, according to her insight, which was no insight at all but simply a fraud to make money. It may be true that she did believe that she was inspired or empowered to see the visions and end of all mortals.

"Mr. Lincoln held to a firm belief all his life; he said to me more than once: 'Billy, I fear that I shall meet with some terrible end.'

"Lincoln was most emphatically a superstitious man. That ran through his being like a bluish red vein runs through the whitest marble, giving the eye rest from the weariness of sameness. The sharp contrast gave beauty to both white surface and bluish red veins.''

The Lincoln family, it is almost certain, held a number of séances in the White House. The president's interest in a world beyond the physical might well have been heightened by the fact that his beloved son, Willie, died of fever in the middle of Lincoln's first term. In fact, Willie's spirit has also been reported in the White House. Another son, Pat, had died earlier, and Lawrence has written, "Lincoln during his own life time claimed to receive regular visits from his two dead sons, Pat and Willie."

In the *Encyclopedia of Psychic Sciences*, Nandor Fodor refers to an article published in the Cleveland *Plain Dealer* to the effect that Lincoln often visited psychics. One of these was a well-known medium, J. B. Conklin. Conklin said the president had visited him often in New York. When Lincoln was shown the article, he did not contradict it; in fact, he did the opposite. He said, "The only falsehood in the statement is that the half of it has not been told. This article does not begin to tell the wonderful things I have witnessed."

Lincoln consulted several of the best-known mediums of the time, and may well have accepted advice from them or from those who purported to speak through them. One writer, Colonel S. F. Kase, has written, "For four succeeding Sundays Mr. Conklin, the medium, was a guest at the Presidential mansion. The result of these interviews was the President's proposition to his cabinet to issue the [Emancipation] Proclamation."

A young medium, Nettie Colburn, is described as going into trance, approaching the president with closed eyes, and addressing him for an hour and a half, urging him to free the slaves.

"Those present," Colburn wrote some thirty years later, "declared that they lost sight of the timid girl in the majesty of the utterance, the strength and force of the language, and the importance of that which was conveyed, and seemed to realize that some strong masculine spirit force was giving speech to almost divine commands. I shall never forget the scene around me when I regained consciousness. I was standing in front of Mr. Lincoln, and he was sitting back in his chair, with his arms folded upon his breast, looking intently at me. I stepped back, naturally confused at the situation, not remembering at once where I was. It took me a moment to remember my whereabouts. A gentleman present then said in a low tone: 'Mr. President, did you notice anything peculiar about the method of address?'

"Mr. Lincoln raised himself, as if shaking off his spell. He glanced quickly at the full-length portrait of Daniel Webster that hung above the piano, and replied, with marked emphasis, 'Yes, and it is very singular, very!' "

At the time, great pressure was being exerted on Lincoln to defer enforcement of the Emancipation Proclamation; Lincoln said it was taking all his nerve and strength to withstand this pressure. But he did—and séances may very well have influenced his decisions.

IV
RETURN THROUGH MUSIC

22
BELITA ADAIR—HER FIRST PIANO TEACHER, SHE SAYS, WAS BEETHOVEN

The next two chapters concern the experiences of Belita Adair, a beautiful, blond woman of twenty-three. She looks like a Shirley Temple who never grew up and speaks in the voice of a ten-year-old girl—but what she says has the threads of wisdom running through it.

Belita does a great deal more than talk—in fact, she speaks rather reluctantly. She plays the piano and sings. Although she says she has never taken any sort of music lessons, her performances are of professional quality; some judges say her technique is extraordinary.

Belita's music-making *should* be extraordinary. Her mentors, she says, include such people as Beethoven, Chopin, Liszt, Mozart, Debussy, Bach, and—to be discussed in the next chapter—Elvis Presley.

Belita started playing the piano when she was two. Her two sisters, who were considerably older than she

Belita Adair at age five

was, had taken piano lessons at school. But neither had talent for, nor cared about, the piano. When Belita was just beginning to walk, she would stand by the piano and reach up and touch the keys. Before long, she had climbed up onto the bench. Her sister, Tatiana, whom the family calls Tania, says "We didn't think very much until she crawled up there."

Soon, without any instruction, Belita began playing. She played, she told me, for her fairy friends: "I saw the fairies, and they told me the little pieces I could play very well. They were very simple pieces at first."

Did Belita see the fairies as she sees living people, or did she see them in her mind? "Both ways," she says. "Sometimes they came out very strongly in the physical. They were beautiful little things. They were dressed in flowing outfits. And sometimes they flew. And then there were the little ones in more solid dress."

"We thought she was just another musical prodigy," her mother, Stephanie Adair, told me. But when Belita was about seven years old she began singing in foreign languages, and the family realized she was a medium. And—if we assume that this is all true—a very special medium. The little girl said she was seeing such notables as Beethoven and Chopin, and began playing what seemed to be original pieces in those composers' styles.

Her sister Tania, it seemed, was also a medium, although not a musical one. She and Belita began to speak in foreign languages at the same time.

"I was outside," Tania told me, "doing some yard work, and all of a sudden I started speaking in a foreign language. I came in and I told Belita, and the same thing happened to her."

Since then, the sisters say they have carried on conversations with many dead people in their native tongues—Spanish, French, Chinese, and many others, often in special and outdated dialects and accents.

Belita was studied extensively by Andrija Puharich, the physician, scientist, and parapsychologist most widely known for his association with psychic Uri Geller. A lengthy article on Belita, written by James Crenshaw, appeared in the May 1978 issue of *Fate* magazine. Crenshaw wrote:

"Some of the languages have been identified by experts. In 1977, Dr. Puharich arranged for Belita, with her mother and Tania, to fly to England for a series of tests. . . . He confirmed that some of the xenoglossy [speaking in languages not normally known to the speaker] tests were impressive, although a Tibetan expert who attempted to converse with Belita decided that her responses were more imitative than conversational.

"However, every other language tested by the experts 'came through fine,' Puharich reported. One example was her conversational demonstration of a thirteenth-century dialect of southern France, attested to by a French linguist who spoke with her. . . . I [Crenshaw] heard Belita sing and play selections that she said were from a Chinese opera. They sounded very Oriental. Dr. Puharich told me that an expert recognized versions of Chinese that were spoken both in ancient and in more recent times.

" 'This distinguished linguist informed me that, no matter how much this girl had been exposed to Chinese, the way she articulated the words and expressions that came through her could not be imitated by a Westerner,' declared Puharich."

Crenshaw said that a rabbi he knows asked Belita, who is not Jewish, to sing in his temple. "It was unbelievable," the rabbi told Crenshaw. "She somehow brought forth our feelings, created our own music, our own expressions. . . . I asked her, 'Where did you get those words?' and she said, 'I don't know. They come to me.' She used words in Hebrew that are not in the daily language. They were more like words we say in our daily prayers. The language was biblical Hebrew. I can't understand how she got some of those words."

When Belita was in her teens, her mother had her tested at various universities. It was not, apparently, a happy experience.

"She didn't like being treated as a guinea pig," Stephanie says.

"A lot of the professors," Belita says, "don't want to focus on a religious aspect—you know how colleges are. So I just throw up my hands in the air."

(Which reminds me, I recently met a young woman in a psychic study group who was a college student. I asked her what college, and she said Harvard, with an almost penitent air. "I thought most people were proud to go to Harvard," I said. She smiled apologetically. "It's so left-brain," she murmured.)

In any case, I contacted two people at California universities who had tested Belita, and neither were impressed with her. One was a well-known parapsychologist whose work can hardly be called excessively left-brain.

"I thought it was a very sad case, indeed," the parapsychologist told me. "The mother is doing all of this to make something of her daughter. She's got the daughter looking like an ingenue. She had her dressed up in a little girl's skirt and low-heeled shoes, and it was grotesque." She said that she does not think Belita is for real.

Earl Blew, a retired professor in the music department at Stanford, also had nothing to offer that Belita might be inclined to put in a résumé. "If what she produced on the piano after those so-called séances is Beethoven, it's no Beethoven I ever had anything to do with," he said. "She did something I think she derived from Beethoven in some manner or other, and also from Chopin. Neither one of them was stylistically convincing."

I asked Blew if he noticed anything startling in the way she played, considering she supposedly never had a lesson in her life.

"In professional terms, no," he replied. "She was nowhere in the league of a very gifted child prodigy. What she was able to do was pleasant enough. More than the ordinary person would expect to do, but not in line with anything like some of the child prodigies that are around."

I mentioned that Belita had also been tested in Stanford's Languages Department, and he replied:

"I was told by a couple of men in the Languages Department that what she did with languages was not impressive either."

Another music expert had a different view of the matter. The late Robin Sanders-Clark, a friend of Crenshaw, was a conductor in England, Denmark, and the United States. He conducted the 20th Century–Fox Symphony Orchestra in a film called *Unfaithfully Yours*, starring Rex Harrison. Harrison played the part of a British symphony conductor, and Sanders-Clark showed him how to act like one in front of the orchestra.

"With the understanding that the young lady has had no musical training whatsoever such as harmony and counterpoint or voice, I think this is an extremely interesting case." Sanders-Clark told Crenshaw in the *Fate* article, "I am particularly impressed with her technique. If it is correct that she has had no lessons, I cannot see how she can play the way she does. She has an amazing technique, really fantastic."

Sanders-Clark said he had no way of judging her claim that her compositions came from dead composers. "They may, they may not," he said. "If they are improvisations, they are magnificent, I would say. It is a hard thing to do, to improvise like that. It is almost incredible without any piano lessons whatsoever. It couldn't be normally produced, in my opinion."

Aside from his admiration for Belita's technique, Sanders-Clark thought her Chopin sounded more like Chopin than her Beethoven sounded like Beethoven. Her Bach, however, greatly impressed him. Crenshaw wrote in his *Fate* article:

"When he asked her to play something by Bach we were both astounded. He declared it was virtually perfect in style and form, with the inclusion of a typical recitative. Yet we were told the piece had never been heard before—on Earth."

Belita was born in the Los Angeles area and lived there with her family till she was fifteen. Her father, Burton Adair, now deceased, was a dentist. Her mother, Stephanie, was born in the United States and is of Austrian descent. Stephanie's mother, also named Stephanie, was born in Salzburg, Austria. There is a Gypsy strain in the family.

Belita's mother was a professional figure skater. She appeared in such shows as "Holiday on Ice" and toured Europe. The two older sisters, Tania and Gioia, were both professional ice skaters.

When Belita was in her mid-teens, she decided she wanted to live in Las Vegas, which seems an odd place for a person of her spiritual orientation. The entire

family, except for Gioia, a married sister, moved there
with Belita and lives there now. When I asked Belita
what attraction Las Vegas had for her she replied, "I felt
a real pull to come here, a real vibration. Aside from
the flashy things, the crazy things that go on here, there
really are a lot of nice people. It's a quiet city, with the
desert atmosphere and the mountains. There are two
sides to the city."

Belita has a voice range of five octaves. It is startling
to hear this young woman with an almost piping
speaking voice suddenly sing in a deep bass tone. She
can also sing high soprano. The extraordinary voice
range seems to date from a time when Belita, still quite
young, had laryngitis. According to Tania, "She
couldn't talk, and she went to the piano to play healing
music for herself, and she started singing."

Stephanie says, "I was doing dishes, and I said,
'Who's singing in there?' I knew it couldn't be Belita,
because with the laryngitis she couldn't even talk."

"Something completely took over," Tania says.

"She was completely healed that day," Stephanie
says.

Crenshaw's wife, Brenda, was present when Crenshaw was conducting this interview. She is a psychic,
and she remarked, "They were working on the voice-
box."

Belita says the languages started coming when she
was about eight. "At first, I was playing just the music
of different nationalties. Then I started to sing in the
languages."

She says she does not speak these languages; they just
come to her spontaneously as she sings.

Belita says she has many spirit guides, but the chief
one is a Persian who lived a thousand years ago in the

city of Persepolis. As an example of other guiding spirits, she says, "I was playing in a hotel here and an Egyptian lady came in. I meditated a minute and asked for one of my guides to help me. I played for her and sang. She asked me to sing the next night and I had to call on the same spirit to come back."

Belita says the first composer who made contact with her was Beethoven. She says she can see him, that he enters her body and plays new compositions on the piano.

"He transfers himself from the light realm into this dimension," she says. "He takes the music from the macrocosm and brings it to me, and I'm able to bring it into manifestation on this plane of existence." Sometimes, she says, other people can see him. "The composers come into my body. They use the house, as you might say. I sit back and let them overshadow me. I could start with one, and without my even knowing it a different vibration might come in. Someone entirely new might come through. But Beethoven is the main one.

"From my earliest days," she says, "I could hear music vibrating down to me. Everyone is born with this thing, but we stop it. We are told to look outward. We all have this within us, but I do not shut it off."

During an interview with James and Brenda Crenshaw, Belita held what some psychics might call a séance, but she said, "It seems like I'm always in a trance state. There's no going into it or coming out of it. I feel like a beautiful light comes over my body, and this is the presence of the person. And they just sing or play through me and their voice just seems to come out."

She said that Beethoven was there and had brought

Chopin with him. She described Chopin as follows:

"He's in a purple velvet suit today with a lot of lace around. He always looks so beautiful. Beethoven's hair and eyes and face are light, Chopin's hair and eyes are darker, and his face is thin. They're just looking around. I'm sure they enjoy being spoken about."

Tania interjected, "They are always looking for someone to channel them—writers, poets, artists—all of them."

Belita then played a piece of music in Chopin's style. "Chopin has stretched my hands," she said. "He changes my hands when he wants me to reach an octave."

When she finished playing, she spoke with a slight accent, purportedly Chopin's:

"I have remained in the body for a minute to tell you this song is about a soul's longing for God and how the soul finds its radiance within a note of music. How it is like the shadows of his spirit as the notes from heaven cascade down the stairway to Earth. And if we can catch these reflections we become the thing reflected, and like a gigantic pool of spirit, this music—like a vast sea—its tide caresses a man's soul if he would only open himself to it."

After a ten-second pause, Belita said in her normal voice, "Oh, so pretty."

Belita sent me a videotape of herself being interviewed on television, and she also performed. There were parts of four different programs on the tape. One of the emcees was actor Richard Kiley, who is best known for originating the role of Don Quixote in *Man of La Mancha*.

"Perhaps," Kiley said, "we're on the threshold of a

new stage in our evolutionary development."

Belita was truly startling, strangely compelling to watch in performance. With a friend who was also watching the video tape, I mused at her immature, little girl voice and manner, and how she seemed to take on entirely different personae as she played and sang.

"She's like in a dream world, frozen in time," my friend said. "I can't picture her ever growing up. What would she gain by growing up? She's gone beyond all of us already."

23
BELITA ADAIR AND
ELVIS PRESLEY

Belita Adair may, many have said, have had contact with the spirits of Beethoven, Mozart, Bach, and other greats of musical history, as described in the preceding chapter. But there are all kinds of music, and there is testimony that musical figures of a quite different sort can also communicate through Belita. For example, Elvis Presley.

Witness to the following incident was George Arnold, a theatrical producer based in Las Vegas, where Belita and her family live. Arnold started as a skater and starred in a number of ice shows. Then he began producing them, which he still does. He has produced other types of shows too, in such places as the Riviera, Canada, and Japan, and for such people as Marlene Dietrich, Harry Belafonte, and Andy Williams.

Arnold has known the Adairs for many years. His mother was a friend of Belita's mother, Stephanie.

Elvis Presley

Stephanie was a figure skater who appeared in a number of notable ice shows and once skated in one of Arnold's revues. Belita's older sisters, Tania and Gioia, were also professional skaters. Surrounded by skaters, Belita became pretty good herself as a child, and sometimes appeared with her sisters in smaller shows.

Arnold told me: "Her mother asked if I could put her in my new show. She was awfully young, but I said I'd talk to her. [She may have been younger than he realized; she was only fifteen.] We had an open audition to which eighty girls came. She had to be hired officially by the owners of the show. I was horrified to put Belita up there, because she'd never had any experience as a showgirl. With no experience, how she got into the positions I have no idea, but the head of the entertainment department of the hotel hired her the first one.''

The show was at the International Hilton, where Presley had appeared many times. They went into rehearsal. The costumers used rooms below the stage area. Belita was down there to be fitted and felt a strange attraction to the place. Arnold, who met Presley a few times, recalled that Presley often used those rooms for dressing and rehearsing. There was a piano that Presley sometimes used to practice with his musicians and on which he would sometimes accompany himself as he informally entertained his entourage.

"Belita had a yearning to go to this downstairs dressing room," Arnold recalled. "I don't think she knew beforehand that Presley had any connection with the place. She didn't know that he had a dressing room there. For all she knew, he dressed in his suite. She was just drawn to that piano, which was in the room adjoining where he changed his clothes.

"Normally, I wouldn't take a girl away from the stage area during a rehearsal break. The choreographer might suddenly want her for something. But I was the producer so I could do what I wanted, and Belita had the desire so badly to go into that room where the piano was that I took her.''

Arnold said Belita immediately went to the piano and sat down. Then, "She just went into a trance, a very deep trance. Elvis Presley apparently came to her, used her. She played a song that he apparently was writing in his head, and she was playing the piano and singing lyrics. At that time Elvis Presley had just recently died. She was speaking in his words; she sang the song in his voice. He sang about how sorry he was that he defiled his body, that he couldn't do what God had wanted him to do on this Earth and gave him the talent to do. Because he had defiled his body he couldn't reach the people he wanted to reach, the people who were his followers or who just liked to hear him.

"While she was singing, her face changed. Her nose changed. It turned white and became Elvis Presley's nose, in order to reach the tone that he would sing in. Her nasal quality had to change because Elvis sang in falsetto, which I believe must have come from his nose or that area someplace. He sang very beautifully when he did a falsetto. Her nose changed into a sculptured Elvis Presley nose in front of my eyes. It became white as if the skin had become taut.

"The words that were coming out were very, very religious. She was singing words like 'holy' and 'glory.' Then as she got more into the song, more into the holy part, she still kept the beat going that Elvis Presley had. It was very distinctive. Elvis had the most sympathetic and the most wonderful voice. He was able to go very softly and then into the rock. Well, she did all of that, but with the lyrics of the religious, saying how happy he was where he was, things she couldn't have made up, impossible for her to make up.

"She couldn't have made them up as rapidly as they came out of her mouth. And they rhymed. It was a song, just as I would put into a show. They came out that way—not as a speech, not as poetry—they came out as a song. The words were so impressive because he was so regretful of what he did to himself. And then how happy he was where he was, more happy than he was here. His only regret in leaving so soon was that he couldn't have stayed on and helped people. He did all that in a kind of soft rock tempo—almost a spiritual song, very spiritual. And yet he kept it in the Elvis Presley style. It would go very low and then very high.

"I was in shock. It was eight years ago but I can remember it as though it was yesterday. The costume women were looking out from behind the costumes. They were spellbound too.

"After it was over, she stopped with her eyes closed and put her hands folded on her lap, bowed her head slightly, and was in that position for a good half a minute. I didn't talk to her while she was there like that, like she was in prayer. But I don't think she was, I think it was just a case of her coming out from the influence. I didn't want to say. 'That was great.' I believe she was exhausted. She doesn't do a lot of talking, anyway. I didn't talk to her until afterward. Then I said, 'How could you do that?' And she said, 'I didn't do it. That was Elvis. I cannot take the credit for that.' "

Although Belita was very young, Arnold said, she had an extraordinary influence over her fellow cast members. "Every time we had a rehearsal break," he said, "the showgirls and boys would gather around Belita like she were a queen or something. They would sit on the floor and she would sit on a chair, and they would just be baffled by what she was telling them. They would rush in a circle around her, and she would talk. These other girls were very experienced in show business. You can't fool them, and they don't want to be fooled. But they were mesmerized by her.

"I don't know what she would tell them. They would ask her questions about philosophy, I think, about their own personal lives. I think it was auras—she could see their auras. But she was so quiet and soft-spoken you could hardly tell that she was speaking. It wasn't like some lecture tour.

"I can tell you, that Belita is something else!"

24
ROSEMARY BROWN AND LISZT— AS WELL AS CHOPIN, BEETHOVEN, BACH, BRAHMS, AND OTHER FRIENDS

When Rosemary Brown was seven years old, she saw a vision of a very old man with white hair, wearing what she took to be a long, black dress. She later realized the "dress" was a cassock, a clerical garment, and the old man was composer Franz Liszt, who had become an abbé in his later years. He had been dead almost half a century.

"When you grow up," he said to her, "I will come back and give you music."

Brown related in one of her books, *Unfinished Symphonies*, that she was not frightened, or even startled, at waking up in the early morning to this apparition. "I had been accustomed to seeing discarnate beings since I was a tiny child," she wrote.

Brown grew up in a drab, working-class neighborhood in London. She got married, had two children, became a widow, and barely made ends meet by work-

Johannes Brahms

ing in the kitchen of a school. She was very psychic; she learned early in life to be very careful about revealing the things she casually saw and knew.

In 1964, when she was in her forties, Brown said Liszt appeared again. In the time between his appearances to her, she realized who the visitor of her childhood was, having seen pictures. "There is, after all," she wrote, "no mistaking Liszt for anyone else, especially when he was an elderly man with long white hair and wearing the sombre robes." She had taken piano lessons for three years and could find her way, although not particularly skillfully, around the keyboard.

On that day in 1964, while playing the piano in her home, Brown suddenly lost control of her hands. Looking up, she saw Liszt guiding her fingers over the keys.

Since then, Brown has turned out an astonishing number of pieces—in the hundreds—in the style of great composers who are long dead. For Liszt, she says, brought along friends, including Chopin, Bach, Schubert, Beethoven, Debussy, Brahms, Grieg, Berlioz, Schumann, Rachmaninov, Monteverdi. She claims that she has heard the finish of Schubert's "Unfinished Symphony." "Schubert let me hear it by telepathy," she wrote. "It is very, very beautiful."

Brown began to demonstrate her strange abilities to psychic groups in the London area. Soon, at the urging of her dead mentors, she went public. Their purpose, she said, was not so much to give more music to the world as to demonstrate to mankind that death is not the end to the individual personality. She appeared on such media as the BBC, which made a film of her, and American TV programs such as "60 Minutes." Newsmagazines such as *Time* and *Newsweek* published surprisingly serious, respectful articles about her. Not all of the reaction was positive. Irving Kolodin of the *Saturday Review* wound up his assessment of her work as follows:

"Allowing for the trillion-to-one possibility that what Miss [sic] Brown says happened did happen, and that she was receiving musical messages from the spirit world, the final conclusion must be that not one of the composers has had a new idea or a worthwhile thing to say in the decades (centuries in the case of Bach) since he last had the opportunity to convey his thoughts on paper."

Frédéric Chopin

Skeptics notwithstanding, Brown became, in a limited way, world famous.

How do the composers direct her? It varies, she wrote. "Liszt controls my hands for a few bars at a time, and then I write the music down. Chopin tells me the notes at the piano and pushes my hands onto the right keys. If it is a song, Schubert tries to sing it—but he hasn't got a very good voice. Beethoven and Bach prefer to have me seated at the table with pencil and paper; then they give me the key, the left hand and the right hand."

Brown's relationships with her spirits went beyond mere musical drudgery. She was not just a convenient

Music written in the hand of Rosemary Brown

amanuensis; they took an interest in her life. She wrote in *Unfinished Symphonies* that Chopin, while giving her music, once suddenly stopped and warned her with some agitation that her daughter had left the bathwater running upstairs and that a flood was about to ensue if something wasn't done forthwith.

She said Chopin also went to concerts she gave, to provide moral support.

Did the composers all learn English in their new lives, or was Brown a polyglot? She always had the ability, she said, to discern the meaning of spoken or written languages she never studied. She told of a childhood school experience when she was able to read the Italian printed on a postcard, causing something of a contretemps with her confused teacher. (Her son, Thomas, has the same ability, she said. She took him with her when he was thirteen and she was being tested by professors at the Department of Parapsychology at the University of Utrecht in Holland. Although he was in a room where everyone was speaking Dutch, he could understand everything they were saying.)

According to Brown, the composers appeared in a variety of dress, as one would in physical life. For example, once Liszt had identified himself by appearing as an old man in a cassock, he became much younger, dressing in clothing of our own time, often quite fashionable. She believes he appeared as the aged Abbé Liszt at first because she would not have recognized him as a handsome young man. She added, "He loves to watch television and on occasion goes shopping with me. Once he flipped an apple out of my hand because he thought I was eating too much."

Beethoven, wrote Brown, is no longer deaf. "He seems about thirty-five and he hasn't got that crabby look any more."

Concerning Schubert: "At first he wore his eyeglasses so I would be sure to recognize him. Now he doesn't wear them at all."

And Debussy: "I think he's what you would call a hippie type. Sometimes he comes in very bizzare clothes. He tells me he does much more painting than music now and he's shown me some of his paintings, which are most beautiful. I think what you'd call impressionist style."

Often she talked with her musical friends—particularly with Liszt—about wider subjects "like the purpose of life, and metaphysics."

As an accomplished psychic, Brown seems to have many visitors from the other world, not all of them famous composers. Many are ordinary as the rest of us. And some are famous in other ways. She says that Liszt brought Einstein to see her, and she has had contact with the physicist many times since. He tries to give her abstract ideas, but she has difficulty comprehending them.

Evidence of Brown's psychic abilities is manifold, but a rather convincing public example was published in the British newspaper the *Daily Mail* by reporter Vicki Mackenzie, and was quoted by Brown in her book *Immortals by My Side*:

"Towards the end of my interview with Rosemary Brown, Rosemary told me she could see a woman standing near me. As Rosemary began to describe this woman, small, dainty, with a round face and an un-English accent, I thought it sounded rather like my Czech aunt who had died a couple of months beforehand. Apparently this woman was dressed in a rose-colored, crepe-de-chine, waisted dress with a camelia on the collar. However, since I had only met this aunt about ten times during my whole life, I would not really be sure whether it was her or not, although I did know she was always very fond of me, just as Rosemary told me she said.

"Rosemary then told me that this woman was saying something about a large ring with a big stone she had had, although never wore. She was giving details, too, of some miniatures that she had of some of her family. Rosemary drew with pencil and paper what she had

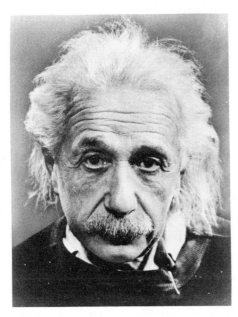

Albert Einstein

gathered was the size of them. And there were other messages of love and of a personal nature which tallied exactly with my experience of that time.

"That evening I rang my uncle, my deceased aunt's husband, and asked him about the ring and the miniatures, which, of course, I had never seen or known about. He was amazed and said that there were in fact two rings, each with a large stone which my aunt had never worn because she felt they were too large for her small hands. And there were three miniatures standing in a glass case containing pictures of my aunt's cousins, miniatures two inches high, exactly the same size as Rosemary had drawn them. When I mentioned the dress, my uncle thought for a moment, then said she had worn a waisted dress with a white camelia on the collar, long before I was born."

Brown has drawn the favorable attention of many

accomplished—even famous—music men. Leonard Bernstein has seen her many times. One time, she related, he commented to her that Chopin had been a sexy man and asked if he still was. She said she'd never noticed, but "in any case, he would not be like that now," since "sex is a physical aspect of life which would hardly manifest itself in a nonphysical being."

(This may be only Brown's opinion. John Lennon, in some of his channeling, indicates that he still enjoys an active, even glamorous, sex life. Carole Lombard is one of the names he drops, saying Clark Gable won't mind since he's already reincarnated in the Far East. Brown said Lennon came to her—see Chapter 12—but he apparently kept discreetly off that subject with the decorous Rosemary.)

Expert opinion on Rosemary Brown ranges from guarded to enthusiastic, although there are also such negative estimates as that of composer-critic Virgil Thompson, who said, "I find far more resemblance in one of her compositions to another than I do to the composers who inspired them."

Many of the more positive judgments refer to Rosemary's being far from an accomplished musician. She had only the most rudimentary musical education and was a poor to average piano player. She herself said she believed she was chosen by the dead composers not only for her abilities as a medium but also because she had just enough musical knowledge to carry out her function and still have it be believable to others.

An example of this point of view was this statement by André Previn, the composer-conductor:

"Some of the music I would be willing to accept as third-, fourth-, fifth-rate Liszt. I think it is music the composers themselves would probably have discarded happily or forgotten about willingly. Of course, the amazing thing about all this is that to write parodies of any kind, whether this is good or worse or possibly better, [it] takes quite a bit of musical education. For someone who does not know the simple vocabulary, the hieroglyphics that constitute notating music, it's damn difficult to write that stuff down and have it even be as simplistically sensible as it is."

An even more definite opinion was expressed by Hepzibah Menuhin, a pianist of a status approaching that of her famous brother, Yehudi. She said: "I look at these manuscripts with immense respect. Each piece is distinctly in the composer's style. She is obviously a psychic person and can plug herself into these influences. How it happens, I don't know."

Richard Rodney Bennett, a respected British composer, said: "A lot of people can improvise but you couldn't fake music like this without years of training. I couldn't have faked some of the Beethoven myself. Even if some of the pieces are bad, that doesn't mean anything. I produce lots of lousy pieces."

Bennett made an interesting technical observation. "One tends," he said, "to write piano music for the size of the hand one has. I have a very large extension between my first finger and thumb, and I tend to write things with extraordinarily long stretches. One does it instinctively. I've noticed that in her things various composers, for instance the Brahms, is always for an enormous hand. The Brahms B Flat Minor Waltz which she has is written for an extraordinarily large hand. Brahms had enormous hands."

One of Brown's most enthusiastic adherents is a concert pianist named Stewart Robb, who lives in southern California. Robb is not only a recognized musician and author, but he is also very much involved in parapsychology. When Brown came into public view in the late 1960s, the Parapsychology Foundation of New York sent Robb to England to investigate her.

Robb was completely convinced. "Lots of musicians," he told me, "can sit down at a piano and improvise in the style of Beethoven or Chopin, but they can't do the sort of thing that comes through her, because it's highly organized music, structured the way a great composer plans it."

Robb considers himself difficult to fool, and cites an example from the 1930s, when he was accompanying a fellow Canadian, violinist Bohdan Hubicki. Fritz Kreisler, the famed violinist-composer, claimed to have found lost manuscripts by such Baroque composers as Pugnani, Corelli, Tartini, and others. These works received great publicity, and the two young Canadians often played the music at concerts. But, Robb says, "When I sat down to accompany Hubicki, I said, 'This is very nice music but it's not in the style of Corelli or Tartini.' I had long been a lover of baroque, and it wasn't the real eighteenth century style. One could see it was by a composer who was certainly living today and couldn't get today out of the music he was trying to imitate. And years later, Kreisler let the cat out of the bag, that he had composed the pieces himself. But for quite a number of years those things paraded around under the names of the eighteenth century composers."

Aside from his musical expertise and intuition, Robb had other arguments for the validity of Rosemary Brown's pieces. Robb is an accomplished player of the harpsichord and has made two records on that instrument. He told of an occasion when Rosemary saw a harpsichord. She had never seen one close up, she said. "But she sat down," Robb relates, "and was trying it out when other hands seemed to take over. She seemed to know what stops to use. This was a two-keyboard harpsichord, quite different from a piano, but she was guided right."

On another occasion, Robb was scheduled to discuss Rosemary on a Los Angeles radio program. Psychologist David Viscott, who also happened to be a composer, had been on the preceding program. "When he heard what my program was to be about," Robb says, "he asked if he could sit in. During the course of the discussion, he asked if I had any of Rosemary's manuscript music. I had some photostats and showed them to him. He studied them for a while, and then said he could see that she was not the composer of the music, but was bringing it through from other sources. I asked how he knew that from looking at the manuscripts, and he had a really good Sherlockian comment. He said, 'A composer plans ahead. He knows the notes that are coming and how many notes there will be in a bar. But this is not the case here. When she comes to the last bar at the end of the page there are sometimes too many notes crammed into it, too many for the amount of space she allowed for. She obviously didn't know how many notes were coming."

Robb speaks of a conversation he had with Sir Humphrey Searle, whom he calls the world's leading authority on Liszt, and whom he quotes as saying, "This music is unquestionably from that composer."

Brown profited little from the music, even though

records of the music were produced and her three books about herself and her work were published. "If it were pop," she said, "I'd probably make a fortune."

She now lives frugally in a small apartment in a two-story house in Wimbledon. A small trust fund set up by admirers early on allowed her to leave her job in the school kitchen and devote her time to the music.

A recent supporter is a well-to-do California woman named Peggy Williams, a friend of Stewart Robb's. "I've chosen to subsidize her with a small amount as a memorial to my husband," Mrs. Williams told me. "I've never met her. She writes in response to what I write; she rarely talks about herself. I wish I knew more than I do. I tell her about some little thing I've been doing and she writes in response. She writes about me and about my health; she's very concerned about that. She lives frugally over there. She never got her flat over sixty degrees all last winter."

25
ROSEMARY BROWN AND THE COMPOSER WHO DIED IN A CONCENTRATION CAMP

In the early 1980s, British conductor Kerry Woodward, who specialized in opera, was interviewed by Bill Jenkins of KABC, Los Angeles, on Jenkins's radio talk show "On the Line." The subject was Rosemary Brown and an extraordinary experience Woodward had had with her.

Woodward was in America for a stint as conductor of the Akron Symphony Orchestra. He has also conducted for the BBC Symphony, the Netherlands Opera, and the San Francisco Opera. Teaming up with Jenkins to interview Woodward was Stewart Robb, the musician who has investigated Rosemary Brown. Robb made a tape of the interview, and this account is drawn from that tape.

Woodward told a strange tale of a tattered opera manuscript found in 1944 when Allied forces entered the Nazi concentration camp Theresienstadt, in

Czechoslovakia. It had been written by a composer well known in Europe, Viktor Ullmann, a Czech Jew who had died in the camp. The text was in German; its title was *Der Kaiser von Atlantis*—The Emperor of Atlantis. The manuscript was eventually entrusted to a friend of Ullmann's, a Dr. Adler, who lived in London.

"Adler had the manuscript for some twenty years," Woodward said, "and tried to interest people in it, but no one was interested."

In 1974, Woodward returned to England for a visit. He met Adler, who invited him to dinner and later showed him the manuscript. Woodward was interested.

"I studied it for some time," Woodward said, "and I decided there was music of real value here. So I began to work on it and I worked on it for eighteen months to make a performing edition. The manuscript was in terrible condition—tattered, blotted, with many sections crossed out, which I believe was for reasons of censorship. The opera was a diatribe against Hitler and against dictatorship; I think that's the reason for the censorship. It's been difficult to reconstruct the whole story of the opera, and in fact my meetings with Rosemary Brown did help clarify some of that.

"I met Rosemary Brown first in a recording session. A friend of mine, Howard Shelley, a pianist, had asked me to produce a record of him playing the music of Rosemary Brown. I had read a book about her some years back and was interested.

"I met her and was very surprised by this . . . this very ordinary housewife, a very simple lady, quiet, quite unassuming, who sat at the back of the studio just listening to what went on, and didn't really say anything.

Rosemary Brown in 1970, drawing by Elizabeth Parrott

"Among the pieces Shelley was playing was a Brahms intermezzo. I was struck by one passage that didn't quite seem right. I'd been very convinced up to this point by the music of Rachmaninov, Chopin, Debussy, and others. But this section of Brahms . . . I went to Howard and said, 'I think there's something wrong with this.' He said, 'Well, let's ask Rosemary.' He agreed that it didn't quite sound genuine.

"So we went to her and she thought for about five seconds and then said, 'Well, Howard, if you just play the left hand you can rearrange the structure of the chords so that the bottom note will come at the top and you take the right hand and you play it an octave higher for a bar and a half.' So Howard did that and then it was perfect Brahms.

"This made me open my eyes, really, because I saw it happen right on the spot. And this happened again with another piece. She was able to change it convincingly immediately.

"She really has very little knowledge of music. She loves music, but it really goes just about that far. She has practiced the piano, but she really has no natural talent. I have to say that, and she'd probably agree with me.

"She's very poor, and she really needs as much help as people can give her. So I said I would like to help her, perhaps just copy her manuscripts, make them legible and let them be distributed. She thought that would be very nice, so I went to her house for dinner, and I took the opera along, although I hadn't been thinking of the opera when I made the offer. She thought I had written the opera, so she really knew nothing about it in advance. She didn't know it had been written in a concentration camp.

"We talked about the opera over dinner. I had brought the original manuscript with me, and also my own performing edition of it. These remained in my briefcase throughout the whole dinner; there was no way she could have seen them. These were the only manuscripts in existence.

"I said to Rosemary, 'Would you like to see the original manuscript?' I took it out of my briefcase and passed it to her. She held out her hand, and then she withdrew her hand in horror. She said, 'I really can't handle that score. The vibrations are far too powerful in a negative way for me to touch.' And that's how it remained; the score sat on my lap.

"She said, 'I'm getting the impression of a man standing over by the light.' She was sitting alongside of me, and she was pointing to my left somewhere. She said, 'He's rather short, and he has close cropped hair, and he's talking about a concentration camp, talking about the horrors. It's really quite terrible to listen to what he's saying. And now I'm getting a terrible smell.'

"It so happened that I had a packet of cigarettes with me, and she said, 'I would like a cigarette. It's actually the first time I've smoked in twenty years, but the smell of this place is really dreadful.' After some time, she said, 'He's now come over to you and he's trying to thank you for the work you've done.' So it became clear that this was the composer, Viktor Ullmann.

"Then she said, 'Now he's looking very businesslike and he wants you to turn to page 11 in the score.' So I turned to page 11. Page 11 was recitative; the singer is saying a lot of text, and the accompaniment underneath it was originally for harpsichord. The composer had put arrows pointing to certain notes saying that these notes should be played by a violin, a cello, a flute, etcetera. When I had made my edition, instead of writing it for harpsichord I wrote it for orchestra, because he had indicated exactly which instruments he wanted. He said, through Rosemary, please make the section on page 21 the same as page 11. Page 21 was again a recitative, rather similar. This time there was only a harpsichord indicated and no arrows, no other instrument. He wanted me to orchestrate page 21 in the same way that I had orchestrated page 11.

"That was the first thing. Then he said turn to page 54, measure 2, the viola part. The rhythm was written in the score, a half note followed by a quarter note. He said, 'I would like you to reverse the rhythm so it is a short note followed by a long note.' His solution made it then correct.

"He said he would like me to compose the beginning of the trio. There was a page missing, and I had written something of an introduction but I had not made it elaborate since I did not want to tamper really with the music, or as little as I needed to. He asked me to compose the beginning. I said I really am not a composer, although I've studied composition. He said 'Don't worry, it will come to you.' He said I would find the material in the trio with which I could compose it.

"There were other sections he wanted me to change. One was the Aria of Death. There was a middle section in this in which he had only scored the harpsichord. He gave me instructions that it should be for flute, muted trumpet, muted strings, and a bell. The bell should sound not at regular instances but rather freely, like a funeral bell. There were many other things.

"All this time, Rosemary really couldn't see the manuscript.

"I went away and worked at his suggestions. I came back about two weeks later to have them checked. On the day I was due to meet Rosemary, I realized I had not composed the introduction to the trio which he had asked me to compose. I sat down with very little time. As I've said, I'm not a composer, but suddenly, in a flash, I knew exactly what I had to do and I wrote it down. It was done immediately. That was a very strange thing that happened to me. In fact, all the work that I did on this came really quite easily. And I'm not a gifted composer at all.

"So I went to Rosemary, and this is very, very interesting. I think this rules out telepathy, that I am the transmitter of the information to Rosemary. Because when I presented my orchestration to Viktor Ullmann, via Rosemary, he said, 'Yes, you've done very well on this Aria of Death, but I asked you to do it for flute and muted trumpet and you've actually reversed it. I really would like you to put it that way around.' The second thing he said was, 'I think that the string parts are written very well, but you've put the funeral bell on the wrong note. And also, I really wanted that funeral bell set a half tone lower.' I did that, and it was a far more mournful quality than the other.

"I got the Netherlands Opera interested and we did nine performances in Holland in the winter of 1975 and the spring of 1976. I've performed it some fifty times all over the world. The revisions were only a small proportion of the whole opera.

"I'm totally convinced that this is not coming from Rosemary Brown's mind," Woodward said. "She's transmitting information from somewhere. At this point, I really don't know what the source of the information is. I had a long conversation with Beethoven through her, which was quite fascinating, one of the most fascinating conversations I've had with anybody in my life. I felt I was in the presence of a great soul, a great mind. I'm totally convinced. I rule out telepathy. I don't know where the information is coming from. It may be coming from a universal mind. I don't know what's the solution, but I'm totally convinced it's not coming from Rosemary Brown's mind."

V
A COUPLE OF TYCOONS

26
F. W. WOOLWORTH MAY NOT HAVE BEEN YOUR USUAL AMERICAN BUSINESS TYCOON

F ive-and-ten-cent store tycoon Frank W. Woolworth is the subject of two intensely researched books. *Five and Ten*, by John K. Winkler, was first published in 1940. *The Woolworths*, by James Brough, was published in 1982. Both authors went over Woolworth's life with a fine-tooth comb (ninety-nine cents at my local Woolworth's) but I could find nothing about any predeliction for the occult on Woolworth's part. I even wrote to Brough about this possible oversight and received in return a rather curt note to the effect that he himself didn't believe in ghosts.

But a large percentage of the people in Glen Cove, Long Island, believe otherwise. Woolworth owned a magnificent mansion there, and most of the townspeople I spoke to were reasonably certain that the place, Winfield Hall, (Woolworth's middle name was Winfield) is replete with apparitions, ghostly music, unac-

countable voices, and other possibly supernatural phenomena. I learned of Woolworth's ghost from Fran
Tucciardo of Huntington, Long Island. A psychic
working as a hypnotherapist, she had been invited to a
series of séances at Winfield Hall about ten years before
my recent interview with her.

Various entities came through the psychics, Tucciardo told me, although over the years, she has forgotten
who some of the spirits were. But she was told that
Woolworth himself came through her. "I was not
aware of everything that was being said," she told me,
"but I was aware that energy was being channeled
through me. It's like being in an altered state of consciousness; you're there but you're not there. Because of
that, it's difficult for me to remember everything that
went on. It's more what people told me about it. I do
remember that Woolworth was very upset because they
were going to remodel his library and take down the
paneling. That seemed to be the room where he concentrated most of his energy. He told us about secret
passageways underneath the organ. One of the men in
the group followed what he said and went through the
secret passageways."

The séances were organized by Monica Randall of
nearby Oyster Bay, who came with interesting credentials. She is a native of the area, the swank North Shore
of Long Island, where multimillionaires who had
town houses in the city built suburban retreats. Her
mother had been a governess for some of these opulent
families, and Randall was fascinated with their life-
styles. She wrote five books on the great houses on
Long Island, including the 1987 volume called *The
Mansions of Long Island's Gold Coast*. She now lives in

(Photo by Monica Randall)

Winfield, F. W. Woolworth's Long Island mansion

a house in Oyster Bay that has been converted into a museum of artifacts of the affluent.

Randall has had a special interest in Winfield Hall for a long time. When she was fourteen the place so fascinated her that one day she gathered her courage, marched up to the door, and knocked. The lady of the house at that time was a grand dame named Mrs. Richard S. Reynolds (one of the aluminum foil Reynoldses, who had bought the place in 1929). She talked about the ghosts and gave Randall a tour of the house.

The mansion was used as a school from 1964 to 1976. It was called Downs School and specialized in the training of models and airline stewardesses. Randall, who was once a model, taught there for a time. During the time of the séances, in the late 1970s, she was temporary caretaker at the mansion.

She was friendly with the two men who then owned the place, Richard Markoll, who owned a construction company in Europe, and Martin Carey, who among his other attainments was the youngest brother of the former governor of New York, Hugh Carey. In one of her books, Monica says that opera singing brought them together. They were both trained as singers, and were struck with the perfect acoustics of the Music Room. "They were often heard singing into the wee hours of the morning," she wrote.

"Everybody knows the place is haunted," Randall told me. "That's common knowledge. The girls constantly talked about apparitions, and they were pretty consistent. It was a one-year program, so each year you had a whole new gaggle of students from all over, and the stories persisted. They would describe seeing a young woman with reddish blonde hair, wearing a blue dress, crying in front of the fireplace. Some of them picked that up on film. I have some of those photographs on file."

(Unfortunately, she was saving them for one of her own books. It seems my best informants are usually working on their own books!)

"One of the photographs," Randall says, "shows a man and a woman. You don't get details of the faces, you get ectoplasmic forms, the outline in a fuzzy white mist, very clearly two human figures. The school finally closed that room, which had been Edna Woolworth's room. They always saw that ghost in that one room. Edna Woolworth committed suicide. She was one of Woolworth's three daughters. She was Barbara Hutton's mother."

Randall says that during the séances Edna came through one of the mediums and was bitter about the cold authoritarianism of her father. "Everything you read about Woolworth is glossed over," Randall says.

"He was a business genius, but the thing that they never mention is that he was obsessed with the idea that he was the reincarnation of Napoleon. His bedroom was an exact replica of one of Napoleon's bedrooms, and everything in it once belonged to Napoleon.

"He believed in the occult in the extreme, and if you're familiar with the occult, as you go through the house you see an awful lot of symbols in the carvings around the fireplace and along the moldings and the friezes. Carvings of dragons and demonic types of symbols—bats, lizards, cactus leaves."

Randall had a frightening experience at one of the séances. "There were nine of us at that séance," she told me. "One of the men became possessed by F. W. Woolworth, and he started to glare at me. I was at the time living in the house. He said, 'You meddling bitch! Get out of my house!' With that, he lunged for my throat. He never made contact because people grabbed him. And this was a man who was a school teacher who lived out in Port Jefferson, as normal a human being as you'll ever find.

"I became caretaker because my friends had lost their caretaker. People wouldn't stay there. They see people floating through the walls, they hear voices. I was working on my first book and I needed a quiet place to write."

Woolworth built the mansion, a sixty-two-room Italian Renaissance villa, in 1917, after another imposing structure there he had owned burned down. He was to enjoy the place for only two years; he died in 1919 of septic poisoning caused by infected teeth. He was terrified of dentists and refused to see one.

He had started life as a farm boy in upstate New York. When he died, he left a personal fortune of sixty-five million dollars, a lot of nickels and dimes. His wife was born Jennie Creighton, a poor girl he had known in his youth, who never accustomed herself to the lifestyle of the wealthy. They had three daughters.

Drawn to retail trade from his early youth, Woolworth became involved with stores while still a teenager. He got the idea of selling merchandise at a standard low price—first a nickel, then expanding to a dime—and it turned out to be an idea whose time had come. Although while researching this chapter I constantly heard that Woolworth had been a failure most of his life and suddenly hit it big, if you check out the dates you find that he was solidly on his way to fame and fortune by the time he was twenty-seven, a fate most of us would settle for.

Dan Russell, the official historian and the harbor master of Glen Cove, ridicules stories of the haunting of Winfield Hall. When I interviewed him, he was less than complimentary about Randall and hinted her motive was the sale of her books. "It's in the wrong part of town," he says. "It's the other part of town that's haunted."

But an unofficial Glen Cove historian has a different story. Glenn Giwojna is a young man who, like Russell, has conducted tours of the North Shore mansions, including Winfield. "That house is definitely the most haunted house in Glen Cove," Giwojna told me. "Everybody in Glen Cove knows about the Woolworth house being haunted. A lot of caretakers and gardeners and house people who have seen ghosts and heard things have left because of it."

Giwoja had a facinating new can of worms to open. "Woolworth," he says, "was heavily involved with cults and covenants and groups of that sort. He had a sort of satanic group back in the twenties that met in the house. They did various kinds of rituals. The vibes there are so intense! There are a lot of mystical creatures and devils and strange things in the woodwork. It's a very strange house."

Giwojna spoke of an elderly neighbor, a retired plumber, who had often done work at Winfield. "I tried to talk about the house with him," Glenn says, "and he doesn't want to talk about it. He said it's very traumatizing. He'll talk about any other estate, but not that one."

Randall says that while she lived in the house during the 1960s, there was a black mirror in one of the master bedrooms. "And that," she says, "is something you"ll find when there are people who are heavily into the black arts."

Part of the folklore of Winfield is the crack in the face of Edna Winfield in the marble family coat of arms over the fireplace in the entrance hall. Legend has it that the crack appeared at the same time that Woolworth's daughter died in Manhattan, reputedly a suicide. Ray Graham, who has designed show cases for the mansion, told me, "It was as though lightning had hit the main fireplace and a crack came through the daughter's face. This is Belgian marble; you could hit it with a sledgehammer and nothing would happen."

Another tradition revolves around Woolworth's gigantic pipe organ. In its time, according to local legend, it was the largest pipe organ in America. Organ music is reputed to still filter through the mansion—

even though no living human is playing it.

The Woolworth estate is now owned solely by Martin Carey and is leased to the Pall Corporation, which manufactures industrial filters. The estate is used as a corporate headquarters, and the mansion itself is a conference center.

"If you call Pall Corporation," Randall told me, "don't even hint that you're writing about ghosts. They want to keep the place pristine pure. It's a hush-hush thing with them. You're better off talking with the people who work there."

I never put the upper echelons of Pall Corporation to the test, but the secretaries seemed to get a kick out of secret passages, angels on the ceiling, and tidbits of that ilk. "I'm sitting in a room that's supposedly haunted. I haven't had any experiences myself, but that's always been the rumor," one young woman told me over the phone, as a chorus of "ooohs" and a stray shriek rose in the background.

I did call Martin Carey and was surprised when he made no bones about an experience he had had. "I was working in Mr. Woolworth's bedroom chambers one day." he told me, "and I heard music. And there was no trace of music anywhere around. But I could hear faint music that I was unable to trace."

In cases like this, though, there is nothing like a night watchman. They always come through! I spoke to one who discreetly declined to give me his name but had what sounded like the inside word. "I hear things like talking when there's nobody around but me," he says. One night I got up my nerve and opened the door, and it stopped. But when I closed the door they started back mumbling. Two or three guards have heard this. Some people have quit. Sometimes workmen like plumbers have heard it. One got scared and threw up the job. A lot of guards don't like to go over there to Winfield. Now you've got me scared to work over there tonight!''

27

THE RETURN OF THE MAN WHO INVENTED FLORIDA — ALONG WITH A FEW FRIENDS AND RELATIVES

Henry Morrison Flagler started life as a poor boy in upstate New York, and in the great tradition of nineteenth century American capitalism had become extremely rich and reasonably famous by the time he died in 1913.

A man with a natural affinity for money, one of his early good ideas was to team up with a young man named John D. Rockefeller, who wanted to get into the oil business. Flagler, already an established business-man, helped Rockefeller raise the money to found Standard Oil, of which Flagler was the first secretary-treasurer.

Flagler did not have such good luck with his personal life. When his first wife fell ill in the late 1870s he took her to Florida, hoping the milder climate might improve her health. It didn't; she died in 1881. But Flagler was impressed with the economic possibilities of the area and, over a few years, he developed such enterprises as railroads that put Florida on the map. It is said that Miami would have been called Flagler except for the intervention of the modest magnate.

In the meantime, Flagler married his widow's nurse, who later went insane. Flagler, then well along in years, became enamored of a southern belle named Mary Lily Kenan, thirty-seven years his junior. Although he wanted to marry her, in New York it was illegal to divorce an insane person. But where there's a will there's a way, and a cooperative Florida state legislature graciously passed a special, temporary law to make Flagler's love match legal. And that's where this story really begins.

When they were married in 1901, Flagler gave Mary Lily one million dollars and a five-hundred-thousand-dollar pearl necklace. That was just for starters. The next year he built a magnificent marble mansion for her in Palm Beach, which they named Whitehall. Including furnishings, it cost four million dollars and has been judged one of the six most imposing private houses ever built in the United States. In 1960, long after the Flaglers' deaths, Flagler's granddaughter, Jean Flagler Matthews, turned the mansion into a museum. It seems to be haunted.

Charles Simmons, director of the museum for the past eighteen years, told me, "There are certain things that have happened here that could be called unexplainable, and that's where we leave it—let everybody make up his own mind."

Simmons suspects there is a feud going on among departed Flaglers. Flagler's son and daughter-in-law did not approve of his marriage to the young Mary Lily. They didn't speak much to her.

In the early 1970s, many furnishings and other items

Henry M. Flagler and his wife, Mary Lily

that were associated with assorted Flaglers were
brought back from their various houses to the museum,
and that time, Simmons says, was the heyday for poltergeist activity in the museum. Strange things happened
to displayed artifacts that originally had belonged to
one or another faction of the family. For example, a
pair of silver asparagus tongs that had belonged to a
Flagler who had been antipathetic to Mary Lily was
brought in and put in a locked glass case on the same

shelf as a dressing table set—a mirror, comb, and brush—that had once been Mary Lily's. "Only the curator, Cathy McElroy, and I had keys to the case," Simmons says. "But one day Cathy found the asparagus tongs on the shelf below. There was no way for that pair of tongs to get onto that lower shelf, except we figured that Mary Lily didn't want any of Lamont Flagler's asparagus tongs on *her* shelf.

"Then there was a series of broken plates that is rather interesting," Simmons says. "They were Mary Lily's plates. They were broken, first one, then another, then another. They were in locked glass cases, and the glass wasn't broken—but the plates were. You could say that one broke because of stress points, but two was a little peculiar, and three was real strange. One of them was shattered as though a bullet had hit it. This happened over a period of a month, in the early seventies."

Another parapsychological problem is the trouble with the old locks on some of the old doors, which are opened with old skeleton keys. "We get mad at our keys," Kenneth Jones, assistant director, told me. "When the old keys won't work, we say, 'Cut that out, Mary Lily!' and the key'll work."

Simmons says, "A door would be opening perfectly easily, and then all of a sudden it wouldn't. It was always happening at the damnedest times. At one time, I lived in the building, and Flagler's granddaughter, Jean, was here and I couldn't unlock the front door to let her out. I said, 'I guess your grandfather doesn't want you to leave tonight.' When we went outside we found the handle of the door had been turned all the way around so that it was catching the door. Somebody might have turned it. Except that after I took her home and came back, then I couldn't get back through the door. I had to come in through the watchman's side. This happened to other people, too, and we'd say, 'Dammit, Mary Lily, cut it out!' and then the door would open. And it was funny, it worked.''

Another prime source of ghostly anecdotes is Maxine Banish, who was director of the Historical Society of Palm Beach County. The society had offices in the Flagler Museum, and for a time she lived there with her husband, Stanley, who was property supervisor of the museum. Stanley never had any psychic experiences, but Maxine often had them—at the museum or anywhere else she lived. One of her experiences occurred in one of the museum's ladies rooms.

"The guides wear turn-of-the-century costumes," Maxine told me. "I was washing my hands in a ladies' room and all of a sudden I realized there was a lady standing beside me in a turn-of-the-century gown, with a big hat on. I said, 'Oh, are the guides having their pictures taken today?' Then I stopped, because I could look straight through her. I stood there a moment and then said, 'Oops!' The figure just faded away. Cathy McElroy was curator then and told me the person probably had been a guest when she was alive. It wasn't Mary Lily! I've seen pictures of her.''

Maxine's dog, Lady Brindle, seemed to be having constant psychic experiences when they lived in the museum. "She used to go upstairs and turn to the left to go into the bedroom," Maxine says, "but every so often she would turn to the right and run down the hall as though she were greeting somebody. Then she'd come back wagging her tail.''

Phyllis Guy, one-time curator of the museum, who

(Courtesy the Henry Morrison Flagler Museum)

Henry Flagler's mansion, now the Henry Morrison Flagler Museum

now works in computer development for IBM, told me she had only one psychic experience in her life, and that was when she apparently saw the same woman Maxine did. "It was early in the morning," she says, "when I was the only one working there, and I thought I saw a woman dressed in a turn-of-the-century outfit, and I could see right through her. I turned around again and she was gone. It was not Mary Lily, it was a younger woman."

Who might the mysterious lady be? Some have speculated that it might be Alice Mary Pomeroy, and here the romantic plot thickens. Miss Pomeroy was said to have vied for Flagler's affections before he chose Mary Lily. No sore loser, she later married his brother, Keenan, so she was often around Whitehall.

Other poltergeist happenings include a ceiling lamp that crashed to the floor; the top of a giant urn did the same thing. Simmons has been quoted as saying he thinks Mary Lily caused some of the breakage, offering the following rather chauvinistic rationale: "Men ghosts don't go around breaking plates."

"Things seem to have calmed down in recent years," Simmon says, but adds, "We did have a weird one a couple of months ago—very, very strange. Jean Flagler Matthews was very active in the Episcopal Church of Florida. When she opened the museum the dedication had at least two or three bishops, a procession of the Cross, a house blessing, and, in effect, an exorcism. One of our new guides, who hadn't yet taken our training course and who I don't think knew that much about Mrs. Matthews as yet, was leading a group on a porch on the second floor and turned around, and over their heads in the background she saw a bishop in full garb, with one of those little holy water sprinkling things, going to four points, as when they bless a house. The guide came downstairs and said, 'Are they making a movie today? Are there some actors around?' "

But whatever happened to Henry Morrison Flagler? Doesn't anyone ever see him? Lynn Gardner of Indianapolis, a professional psychic, visited the mansion a couple of years ago, and told me she had definite contact with Flagler.

"He was a very impressive energy," she says. "He was very playful and very proud of what he had done."

Flagler's presence, Gardner says, was very strong in the music room, where he had spent a great deal of time. He also showed great interest in the gardens around the house. "It was very clear that these gardens were very important to him, that he had built them," she says. "And he loved his miniature trains. He laid one of the first railroad lines in Florida. He was like a kid who was amused by toy trains. They were very important to him; he was fascinated by them.

"I also got that he felt very bad about his second wife, who was institutionalized. He provided for her in such a way that if he died her estate would have an incredible amount. Even if he died and lost everything she would never be without.

"Some people were very angry when he divorced her. He felt his heart was with her, but he had to go on living. The people who were escorting me said he and his new young wife had this incredible bedroom, but of course he was quite a bit older. Flagler let out this big guffaw. He said, 'We had a very good relationship that was physical.' It amused him that they thought that because he was old there was nothing there.

"With the servants, he could be like two personalities. He could either bark, or he could be very gentle. There was a lot of spirit energy in the building. This was a favorite place for many people who had worked there or lived there."

An article in the *Miami News* indicates some of the servants might have had contact with Flagler after his death. An elderly night watchman, John Roth, told the reporter he saw Flagler standing only three feet away when he woke up one night in the guard room, just off the main dining room. According to Roth, the ghost was dressed in street clothes, as he looked in pictures taken a few years before his death. He was shorter than Roth expected. Then he was gone, in a flash.

Another night watchman told not only of having seen Flagler but of having carried on conversations with him.

But Gertrude Sammon, a receptionist at the time of the *News* story, said she didn't believe in ghosts. She speculated, however, that there were goblins there. In an Irish brogue, she told of a guard who swore he was attacked by lavender, one-and-a-half-foot goblins who were stealing oranges from the trees in the garden. "Whatever they were," she said, "they weren't leprechauns. Leprechauns wear green, not lavender. Anyway, they're only in Ireland."

VI

THE
LITERARY
WORLD

28
ALLEN GINSBERG HEARS A VOICE

Allen Ginsberg is one of the most popular modern poets, a frequent reader of his poetry at colleges, literary gatherings, and book fairs. His work has a strong mystical element. Ginsberg often refers to an experience he had when he was twenty-two and very much caught up in the work of William Blake, a late-eighteenth- and early-nineteenth-century English artist, poet, and mystic.

Ginsberg has been interviewed many times about this possibly psychic experience, which has strongly influenced his life and work. He has called it a visionary or a psychedelic experience and has said that it completely changed his attitude toward poetry. One account of it appeared in the summer 1965 issue of the *Paris Review,* another in a collection of interviews with poets gathered under the title *Talking Poetics from Naropa Institute.*

Once, in 1948, Ginsberg was sitting looking at and not really reading the page in a Blake book on which Blake's poem "The Sunflower" appeared.

> Ah, Sunflower! weary of time
> Who countest the steps of the Sun;
> Seeking that sweet golden clime,
> Where the traveller's journey is done.

Ginsberg suddenly felt that the poem was talking about *him*. Just as suddenly as he began to understand it, simultaneously he heard "a very deep, earthen, grave voice" in the room intoning the words of the poem. It was no voice he knew and he immediately assumed it was Blake's. The voice, said Ginsberg, "woke me further deep in my understanding of the poem, because the voice was so completely tender and beautifully ancient. The peculiar quality of the voice was something unforgettable because it was like God had a human voice, with all the infinite tenderness and anciency and mortal gravity of a living Creator speaking to his son."

Ginsberg has never quite figured out his mystifying experience, which he termed an auditory hallucination without drugs.

"I heard a voice and went around for weeks and months and years telling people I heard Blake's voice," he said. " 'I heard Blake's voice!' "

29
ARTHUR KOESTLER AND THE GHOST OF HIS HOSTESS'S DERANGED UNCLE

Arthur Koestler, who, as one critic has put it, wrote one great novel and several good ones, had such a wide-ranging intellect that he occasionally wandered away from his areas of expertise.

By his death in 1983 at age seventy-eight, he had written thirty books—six of them novels—concerned with politics, philosophy, and popular science. *Darkness at Noon* was considered to be his masterwork.

Critics offered both laurels and an occasional brickbat. One characterized him as "an enormously intelligent man with a truly amazing power to apprehend knowledge and grasp the gist of quite difficult theories."

A less enthusiastic critic wrote, "Arthur Koestler's forays into the history of science have done little to enhance his reputation, save among those uneducated in science."

Throughout his life Koestler dabbled, sometimes apologetically, in parapsychology. He wrote in his 1980 book *Bricks to Babel*:

"Half of my friends accuse me of an excess of scientific pedantry, the other half of unscientific leanings toward preposterous subjects such as extrasensory perception, which they include in the domain of the supernatural. However, it is comforting to know that the same accusations are leveled at an elite of scientists, who make excellent company in the dock.

"An impressive number of eminent physicists, from Einstein downward, have shown an inclination to flirt with parapsychology; and, as in other subversive movements, the number of fellow travelers exceeds by far that of card-carrying members. Now why should physicists in particular show this proneness to the ESP virus? The answer is hinted at in the autobiographical writings and metaphysical speculations of some of the greatest of them. The dominant chord that echoes through them is a pervasive feeling of frustration, caused by the realization that science can elucidate only certain aspects, or levels, of reality, while the ultimate questions must always elude its grasp—vanishing into infinite regress like images reflected in a hall of mirrors."

Some years ago, however, I attended a series of lectures and demonstrations given by an extraordinary young English psychic named Matthew Manning. At one point, someone in the audience asked Manning how scientists reacted to his powers. The most favorably inclined, he said, were physicists. "I think," he mused, "that so much has happened in their field in the last thirty years that they're ready to believe anything."

One can find little about Koestler's propensity for the occult in the reams written about him, except in a magazine such as *Fate*, which is devoted to parapsychology. One must peruse the writings of Koestler himself to glean hints of such an interest.

Koestler's intermittent experience with the paranormal began at an early age. The only child of a middle-class family in Vienna, he was guilt-ridden, lonely, introspective—just the type to induce poltergeist phenomena. Renee Haynes, editor of *The Journal of the Society for Psychical Research* in London, described such a paranormal incident in her essay, "Wrestling Jacob: Koestler and the Paranormal."

"It occurred in a Viennese pension where he and his parents were living. An only child, nine years old, isolated and full of inner turbulence."

She quoted Koestler as follows:

"I was reading in my room one lonely afternoon when there was a loud report and a hard object hit me on the back of the head. A big can of baked beans that had been standing on the radiator cover had exploded, presumably from the effects of fermentation."

However, Haynes did not readily accept that mundane explanation.

"Do canned beans ever ferment to such a pitch as to become tinned bombs?" she wrote. "Solitude, powerlessness, high emotional tension produce optimum conditions for the release of psychokinesis."

Haynes pointed out that other inhabitants of the pension interpreted the incident as paranormal. Apparently there was a great deal of table tipping being done in this pension, and Koestler reported that from then on he was in much demand at these sessions.

As a young writer, Koestler had an entertaining

brush with the psychic. As a poor emigré in Paris, in flight from the Nazis, he was approached by two Hungarian-born brothers whom he has identified only as Freddie and Theodore. The brothers had established a publishing firm that operated on an unusual principle. Rather than issuing a book and then selling it, they prepared pamphlets that announced a volume as ready for distribution. Only if they found the response adequate did they actually go ahead with the project.

Operating on this procedure, the brothers offered Koestler either an *Encyclopedia of Psychic Research* or an *Encyclopedia of Sex*. He replied that he was willing to do either, or both. Mail-order solicitations, however, revealed that the readers' interest in sex far outweighed their interest in the psychic. So Koestler did the sex book, which was commercially successful and was eventually published in an English translation.

A central factor in Koestler's life and career was his time in solitary confinement in a Spanish prison in 1937, during the Spanish Civil War. From this experience came the novel *Darkness at Noon*. Koestler was an apostate communist, and the book was about an old, prominent Bolshevik, imprisoned by a new generation of communists and forced to confess to crimes against the state of which he is innocent.

In *Bricks to Babel*, Koestler related his recollection, during his three months of imprisonment by the Franco regime, of an episode in Thomas Mann's novel *Buddenbrooks*. In it the character Counsel Thomas Buddenbrook, though only in his forties, knows that he is about to die and becomes entranced by a "little book" that had long stood unread in his library. The book explains to Buddenbrook, wrote Koestler, "that death is not final, merely a transition to another, impersonal kind of existence, a reunion with cosmic oneness." Mann wrote, "There clung to his senses a profound intoxication, a strange, sweet, vague allurement . . . he was no longer prevented from grasping eternity."

Koestler knew that the "little book" was Schopenhauer's essay "On Death and Its Relation to the Indestructibility of Our Essential Selves," and recalling Mann's passage gave Koestler much-needed comfort.

The day after being set free, Koestler wrote Mann, whom he had never met, a letter in which he explained his circumstances and thanked Mann for the comfort the passage had given him. Koestler expressly mentioned the title of Schopenhauer's essay in his letter.

"Thomas Mann's answer reached me a few days later in London," wrote Koestler. "Mann explained that he had read the Schopenhauer essay in 1897 or 1898, while he was writing *Buddenbrooks*, and that he had never wanted to read it again because he did not want to weaken its original strong impact. The day before, however, sitting in his garden, he felt a sudden impulse to read the essay once more, after nearly forty years. He went indoors to fetch the volume from his library; at that moment there was a ring at the door and the postman handed him my letter."

Possibly Koestler's most intriguing parapsychological experience occurred when as a young man he was a guest of Maria Kloepfer, the widow of a German film actor. The house, on the shore of Lake Lugano, was supposedly haunted by an apparition, and there were reports of occasional poltergeist phenomena.

Koestler was working on a novel at the time. His

hostess spent much of her time swimming and sun-
bathing. The house was kept by an elderly maid, and
the only other occupant was an aging dog, Ricky.
Shortly after Koestler's arrival, Kloepfer asked him if he
believed in ghosts. He answered, he related, "with a
joke" and the subject was dropped. But a little later, he
recalled, Kloepfer said, "casually, in her well-bred
manner, that if at night I heard knocking on the walls
I should not worry; she had all her life been plagued by
poltergeists, but they were harmless."

Koestler wrote that one time they were walking in
the woods with Ricky running ahead. "Suddenly
Ricky stopped, rooted to the mossy ground, and gave
out a growl which then changed into a plaintive, long-
drawn howl. Maria also stopped and grabbed my arm.
That alone gave me a start, for she normally avoided
and shrank away from all physical contact. Her face
had changed color in the undefinably painful manner
of a person growing pale under a sunburnt skin, and
the braces on her teeth became very visible. The wail-
ing dog's hair was actually bristling and the whole
scene was so eerie that I felt suspended between horror
and the giggles."

The three turned, Maria barely able to keep from
running home at full speed, the dog by her side. "Now
and then," Koestler wrote, "licking her hand as if to
comfort her."

Back at the house, Koestler wrote, the usually aloof
Kloepfer begged him, "Don't leave me alone, please."
She had a few glasses of wine, which relaxed her, and
then she told Koestler:

"Ricky saw my uncle approaching us. He sometimes
sees him first and warns me."

She told Koestler that her encounter with an uncle's apparition showed him in a triple image—one coming at her from the front and two simultaneously approaching from the left and right. The uncle, who died when Kloepfler was only three years old, had become deranged. Once, left alone with her when she was two or three, he had sexually assaulted her. Following a nervous breakdown later in life, she had undergone psychoanalytic treatment, which had revived the memory of the incident.

"But the revival of this memory," Koestler wrote, "did not cure Kloepfer. On the contrary, it was after the conjuring up of the uncle's ghost that the hallucinations started."

The following day, as they were sitting down for lunch, a large, framed picture that hung on the wall facing Koestler crashed down onto the sideboard below it. Kloepfer, who sat with her back to it, did not move a muscle—she had grown used to this sort of disturbance—but it made Koestler jump. Some yogurt jars that had been standing on the sideboard in various stages of curdling were knocked into disarray, their contents spilled. Koestler found that the picture's wire was not broken and the two hooks on which the painting had been fastened had remained solidly in the wall.

When the maid came in asking what had happened, Kloepfer simply said, "The haunting." The maid answered, "Not again! Now madame will have to go without yogurt for a whole week."

Although Kloepfer enjoyed literary communists as houseguests and had done reading in Marxism, she also was interested in spiritual subjects, and tried to talk with Koestler about such things. Koestler, describing himself as "a prim little materialist" at the time, was fascinated but repelled by these metaphysical ideas.

A week after he left, Koestler reported, the apparition of the dead uncle reappeared on the veranda and Kloepfer experienced something similar to an epileptic seizure. Although this had happened before, this time she was placed in a doctor's care. A few weeks later she was taken to an institution, and within a few months she was dead.

30
THOMAS WOLFE SPRANG FROM PSYCHIC ROOTS— HIS FAMILY COULD SEE THE FUTURE

Thomas Wolfe was a literary phenomenon, a gigantic man who wrote gigantic novels. He turned in one novel that, it is said, even in skeletonized form was twice the length of *War and Peace*. Luckily, Wolfe found a good editor, Maxwell Perkins, who was adept at what some called surgery, but what Wolfe, appreciative though he was, sometimes called "carnage."

Born in 1900, Wolfe died in 1938, shortly before his thirty-eighth birthday. He knew he would die young. In his novel *You Can't Go Home Again*, published posthumously, he wrote:

"Something has spoken to me in the night, burning the tapers of the waning year: something has spoken to me in the night and told me I shall die."

It is apparent from that brief passage that Wolfe was

on and on. He was considered an authentic literary descendant of Walt Whitman. Indeed, hundreds of thousands of high school and college students of a couple generations ago drove their teachers to the brink of derangement by trying to write like Thomas Wolfe.

Wolfe seemed comfortable only when he was writing. His capacity for work and the immense volume of words that poured from him matched his giant frame. Friends urged him to slow his frenetic pace, but he said to one of them, "No, I've got to hurry to get it all down. They say I'll write myself out but I won't live that long."

Wolfe's early demise was not foreshadowed by bad health. He had a gargantuan appetite for life, and his death was unexpected. A cold turned into pneumonia, which triggered the recurrence of an almost unnoticed bout of mild tuberculosis he had contracted in his childhood. The reactivated disease entered his bloodstream and centered in his brain. Within weeks he was dead.

Wolfe's family had come from his native Asheville, North Carolina, to Johns Hopkins Hospital in Baltimore, where he had undergone brain surgery. Doctors told the family he was on the way to recovery. His mother, Julia Westall Wolfe, knew better. Her own life, and those of many of her forebears, had been studded with prophecy, particularly regarding death. Family lore contained many such instances.

Thomas Wolfe's great-grandfather, William Westall, while apparently in good health, foretold his own death the next morning at ten minutes before six to his eldest son, Sam. At precisely that time, he died.

Twenty years later, the author's grandfather, Thomas

C. Westall, a son of William, emulated his father by predicting the hour he would die. And he did.

Julia had many prophetic dreams, although she considered them visions because of their accuracy. As a child she dreamed of the death of her sister, Sallie, and saw her lying on a trundle bed. Later in the dream she saw the trundle bedstead leaning against the chimney in pouring rain. Julia told her mother what she had dreamed. Sallie had been ill, but not, it was considered, dangerously. There was no trundle bed in the house.

A few weeks later, at the suggestion of a neighbor, Julia's father built an old-fashioned trundle bed and put it in the middle of the floor so it would be easier for the family to attend the ill Sallie. A few weeks later, she died in the bed. Shortly after her death, the grieving family was having coffee in the kitchen and Julia happened to open the kitchen door. There, leaning against the chimney in a heavy downpour, was the bedstead, as she had seen in her dream.

Julia had subsequent dreams about Sallie. A few weeks later, Sallie appeared in a dream along with the girls' deceased grandmother. They took Julia along a luminous pathway into what seemed a new, exquisite world. Julia wanted to stay, but Sallie told her she had to return and await her time.

Julia had at least one experience involving the ghostly arrival of a living person, a phenomenon that for some reason seems particularly prevalent in the Scandinavian countries and in the northern midwestern United States, where many people of Scandinavian origin live. Her father, Thomas Westall, had left home one morning to help a relative build a house, and said he would bring back some apples. Watching from the prone to indulge in poetic prose. And he tended to go porch later in the day, Julia saw her father in the distance, with a lumpy white sack over his shoulder. She called to her mother that he was coming with the promised apples, and Mrs. Westall hurried to get supper on the table. Suddenly, Westall disappeared. Hours passed, and the family's puzzlement turned to concern. But late that night, Westall finally reached home, carrying the apples in a white pillowcase. He had stayed to have supper with his kin, he explained.

Thomas was not particularly startled by Julia's strange vision, for he himself had been involved in such psychic experiences. Once, when he was a small boy, his mother found him asleep at home when he was supposed to have gone to church. She decided to let him sleep, to lecture him later. When she went to look in on him again, he wasn't there. Later, he returned home from Sunday school with the rest of the family. He had been with them all the time.

In adulthood, Thomas said he often saw a dual self walking along beside him.

In 1892, when Julia was in her fifth pregnancy, she became ill and did not think she would survive to give birth. But one night, she reported, she felt invisible comforting arms around her shoulders and heard a whispered, "Two, two." From another part of the room, a second voice called, "Twenty, twenty." Frightened, she told her husband. Did it mean she was going to die in two weeks or twenty days? Exactly twenty days after this experience, twin sons were born.

Julia apparently had no premonition that her son, Thomas Clayton, would grow up to be a world-famous author. But she knew in the Baltimore hospital, that his life was at its end. And so did Tom. The last words he wrote, when he was first hospitalized with pneumonia in Seattle weeks before during a tour of the West, were a letter to a friend predicting that he would soon die.

31

DOES THE GHOST OF ELINOR WYLIE HAUNT THE MACDOWELL COLONY?

When one writes about such outré subjects as ghosts, one sooner or later comes up against a phenomenon that might be termed Establishment uptightness.

In preparing *The Ghostly Register*, I came across a fascinating TV station in Portland, Oregon, which seemed to be inhabited by the ghost of a Chinese laundress—not as unlikely as it might sound, since the station's building had once housed an Oriental laundry. A few years ago, the station had actually done a show on its ghost. Several members of the staff, as well as a dowser who claims to have detected the ghost with his rod, gleefully gave me the full story. However, the current manager of the station was very much against further media attention to their otherworldly guest. He conveyed this to me most emphatically through his secretary—he wouldn't come to the phone.

I acceded to his wishes since I already had two good stories in Portland (a university with a singing ghost and a bar where the ghost flushes the toilet in the men's room).

In Newport News, Virginia, a small museum called the Adam Thoroughgood House is replete with apparitions, moving objects, bangs, and crashes. When I was writing a book on the occult several years ago titled *The Ghost Hunters*, the Thoroughgood House's first curator, Martha Bradley, gave me a fascinating account of the goings-on there, as did other members of the staff. But when I wanted to do a reprise several years later for *The Ghostly Register*, the new administrative people denied everything very brusquely. I ignored them, and the Thoroughgood House duly became a stop on *The Ghostly Register*'s itinerary.

A few months before I began this book, I happened to be in Peterborough, New Hampshire, where the MacDowell Colony is located. This is a lovely haven for writers, composers, painters, and other artistes, a place where they can do their things in a sylvan setting— everything gratis. Many famous people have spent time there. A young woman in the office told me, "You ought to write about this place" and told me that the ghosts of Elinor Wylie and Edward Arlington Robinson, and perhaps others, are reputedly still floating around this rent-free paradise. I made a mental note.

A short time later, I was reading John Fuller's 1976 book about a haunted airline (Eastern) titled *The Ghost of Flight 401*. In a seven-page aside, he recalls rusticating at MacDowell and contacting what sounded like Elinor Wylie on a Ouija board. I have met Fuller, and I called him to see if he had any additional information on the experience, but he said he had put it all in the book. Perhaps, he suggested, his Ouija board partners, Bill and Susan Moody, might have something further to say. So I tracked down Susan.

But before this I called the colony itself, and got its director. John Mitchell of Watergate fame could have taken stonewalling lessons from this fellow. He never heard anything about anything like that! He didn't know anybody who would know anything either. He didn't even remember anybody who had ever been at the colony. Finally, he did give me the name of a former director. A judicious choice, because this fellow professed to know even less than the first one.

And so, having made my point about the difficulty we earnest investigators sometimes have in getting by The People in Charge, let us move on to Elinor Wylie.

Poet and novelist Elinor Wylie was the darling of New York literary society in the 1920s. She had a way with the critics. One leading critic, William Rose Benet, became her third husband in 1923. Another critic, Carl Van Vechten, led a torchlight parade through New York City in honor of her first novel. You can't do much better than that.

Wylie had beauty, wealth, social position, and talent, but her external and internal lives were at odds. As one critic put it, her work "conveyed the tension between beautiful exterior and turbulent interior."

"For Wylie," another commentator said, "the gifted individual requires beauty, refinement, and variety, while the world offers commoness, coarseness, and vulgarity."

Wylie wrote many poems at MacDowell Colony.

In *The Ghost of Flight 401*, John Fuller wrote: "I had

not been aware in my two previous stays at MacDowell that there were several ghost stories involving it. One very persistent story involved the ghost of Elinor Wylie. She was constantly reported being seen on the stairways of the main lodge. She was also alleged to be seen in the room she once slept in. . . . Those who later slept in the 'Elinor Wylie Room' would persistently report strange noises and appearances. The reports would come from reasonably sane and sober people."

One evening, Fuller was having a few drinks with some people, including Susan and Bill Moody. Susan was a dietitian at the Colony and Bill was a poet; they lived in a nearby town. The talk turned to the possibility of life after death, and the Moodys suggested they try a Ouija board. The couple took positions at the board. At first the planchette indicated letters so fast it was impossible to record them, but soon settled down. The group began asking questions.

The first question was: "Can you identify yourself?"

The planchette slid to yes.

"Are you someone who was here at MacDowell?"

Again the answer was yes.

The Moodys asked, "Please state whether you were a writer, an artist, or a composer."

The planchette began moving in rather swift circles, then spelled out: POET.

"What is your name?"

The device moved to two letters and stopped: E.W.

"When were you at MacDowell?"

The device moved to the bottom row of numbers and spelled out: 1925-1926-1927.

Fuller immediately checked the wooden plaques on the room's wall, which had the signatures of former guests. He ascertained that Wylie had signed into this building, called the Watson Studio, several times in the mid-1920s.

The question was then asked, "Will you talk to us?"

The board spelled: YES, IF YOU BLOW OUT THE LIGHTS.

The lights in the studio were electric, but it was learned later that during the 1920s kerosene lamps were used. The lights were turned off.

Wylie was asked what were the titles of some of her verse.

The answer was: HELP ME.

No one was familiar with any such title in Wylie's work, and it was asked, "Is that a title, or something you are asking for?"

The device spelled: SOMETHING I NEED.

At this point, the chill in the room seemed to increase. The Moodys stood up, and one of them turned the lights back on. Everyone had had enough.

Susan now works only occasionally at MacDowell. Her regular work is as a librarian in a school. She and Bill are divorced, and he lives in Spain. She was friendly when I spoke with her but reluctant to talk about the experience.

"I remember that the communicator asked us to blow out the lights. We were all aware that there was some call for help there," she says.

"I feel strange about this because since that time I have had a conversion. I feel strange about giving it any credit. I've gotten rid of my copy of John's book, not because I don't love John with all my heart, but because I don't line up with that anymore, such an utterly ungodly thing. In the light of my Christianity, anything to do with the occult is of Satan and not of the Lord," she says.

Although she spends little time at MacDowell now, she says things haven't changed.

"I think there's a sense of presence there," she said. "People feel there are spirits there."

32
ADMIRAL BYRD AND HIS GRANDDAUGHTER

Evelyn Clarke is a granddaughter of Admiral Richard Evelyn Byrd, the famous explorer and twentieth-century American hero.

With a degree from the Boston Museum School of Fine Arts, she is a graphic designer with an interest in being a writer; she has had poetry published. She is also an excellent painter.

Clarke was very close to her grandfather, she told me. He died in 1957, and she says she is still close to him. "I loved my grandfather," she says. "We had a very special relationship. You're the first person I'm going to tell this story to, it's so dear and so deep. I was his favorite grandchild. He always used to call me his little philosopher. He would sit me on the back of his shoulders and we would walk through the woods and groves and talk about nature and, in fact, philosophy. I was only six years old then, but I understood him.

Evelyn Clarke   *(photo by Arthur Myers)*

"The family had a place at a lake in Maine. We'd go down and sit on the rocks by the lake. He would look out at space, and his concentration was so deep. I always knew that when he was looking out across vast spaces that I shouldn't talk to him. I just let him be quiet. We'd walk through the woods together, and he'd hold my hand. We'd identify things in nature together, in a very quiet way. We weren't boisterous. He was a very quiet man. We communicated nonverbally. He seemed to know what I needed and I knew what he needed.

"One time he gave a doll to each of his granddaughters. I have two sisters. They were old-fashioned dolls. Each doll represented one of the characters in *Little*

Women. He gave me mine last, and I thought, I'm not going to get a doll. Then he took me aside and put me on his knee, and he said to me, 'I'm giving you Jo, because someday you're going to be a woman like Jo in *Little Women*.''

In the movie, that was the part that made Katharine Hepburn famous—the intellectual, artistic, independent sister.

"One time," Clarke says, "at our log cabin in Maine I was playing with my doll and the arms came off. I was hysterical. I didn't know what to do. I started crying, crying, crying. I went to my grandfather. He fooled around with it for awhile and put the arms back together again, and then he said to me, 'Lynn, that's what life is for. If things fall apart, you need to find the elastic to put it back together again.'

"He died when I was ten. He was in Boston and I was in Pennsylvania. They wouldn't let me go see him, and I was going crazy because I wanted to see him.''

One of Byrd's greatest feats was spending months in an isolated hut on the Antarctic continent, a self-imposed exile for meteorological and other scientific investigation. He had problems with his gas stove and with the minus fifty- to seventy-degree temperatures. He almost died. He described his experiences in the bestselling book *Alone*, originally published in 1938.

"He had a near-death experience in Antartica," Clarke said. "He was a changed man when they pulled him out of there half alive. My grandfather always had the potential to be highly psychic, but his personality was to throw himself into activity. So until he experienced near-death, he didn't contemplate as a psychic would contemplate.

"He would talk to me about loneliness, about the search for self. He talked about how difficult it was to be famous, because of the lack of privacy. He'd tell me this while we were sitting on the rocks by the lake. Once in a while he would say he felt very lonely.

"It took me something like twenty years to be able to read *Alone*. When I finally read it, I realized that a lot of my poetry is in the same language as his book.

"Since he died, he tends to come to me when I'm doing something very simple, something very mundane—nothing like reading, nothing complicated. The first time it happened, I was in my apartment washing dishes and I felt this chill. It went right up my spine. If I didn't know so much about myself I would have been frightened but I stopped washing the dishes and sat down in a chair and just waited. And my grandfather came to me.

"He walked around me and he put his hands on my shoulders. And he talked to me and he said, 'There is a light beyond us, and you are being guided toward that light. There is no need to be afraid of this light. But you must make sure that you learn how to be receptive to its coming. I'm here to help you do that and to protect you.'

"This has happened several times. I don't see him, but I feel him. He has said, 'You have a very difficult journey because of the depth of your insight.'

"He always comes around me and puts his hands on the back of my shoulders. It's a very precious thing."

VII
AN
ASSORTMENT
OF HEROES

33
WHO GOES THERE?
COULD IT BE
BUFFALO BILL CODY?

A high percentage of ghost stories are, to put it politely, folklore. In this book, I've tried to bring the genre back to the realm of nonfiction, finding witnesses who can give first-hand reports and exercising due caution regarding these reports. However, in historical accounts, the mists of time tend to obscure things a bit, and one must often do with twice- or thrice-told tales.

But the story of the old Pension Building in Washington, time-tinged though it may be, seems too good to leave out of this book, even though it might strain the author-reader contract of willing suspension of disbelief. If these things didn't happen, they should have. And so, with this caveat, let us plunge onward.

Probably few readers have heard of the Pension Building. I worked in Washington on a newspaper and I never did. The old place is somewhat passé. It was

261

opened in 1887, and until 1926 it housed the administration of pensions for war veterans. Later other gov-
ernmental agencies used the building, and in recent
years it has become a museum of the building trades,
called the National Building Museum.

"But we still call it the old Pension Building," Joyce
Elliott, director of publications for the museum told
me. "It's really the most fantastic interior space you
have ever been in. We have this interior courtyard that's
the size of a football field, and it goes up 159 feet at its
highest peak. It has eight of the largest Corinthian
columns in the world in it. We're really talking marvel-
ous space. It's just unreal!"

The idea for the building came from U.S. Quarter-
master General Montgomery C. Meigs. He fancied
himself an architect, although many Washingtonians
considered him simply an eccentric. But he had a habit
of getting his way, and he got the building built, even
though in its time it was often called Meigs's Old Red
Barn. Meigs's detractors relished an anecdote about the
Civil War General Philip Sheridan. When Sheridan
was shown through the building, his guide announced
proudly that the building, composed of 15 million
bricks, was fireproof, to which Sheridan reportedly
replied, "What a pity."

But it was touted as the largest brick building in the
world, and those Corinthian columns were hard to
ignore. Meigs suffered one of his rare compromises on
the columns. He wanted to import solid marble, but the
government wouldn't foot the bill. So he had to settle
for what was euphemistically called simulated onyx.

"The columns are marbleized," said Elliott. "It was
a Victorian technique to paint over several layers. They

(Courtesy National Building Museum; © 1986 Harlan Hambright)

The Great Hall of the old Pension Building

used feathers and different colors to make the things look like marble. The largest columns are each made of seventy thousand bricks that are covered with plaster and terra-cotta, and then they're painted.''

The columns are central to this story. They're also hollow, and that's another point of interest.

In 1893, President Grover Cleveland held his Inaugural Ball in the mammoth structure. The center of attention was Buffalo Bill Cody, Indian fighter and showman, who still had a long trail awinding before he was to cash in his chips; he died in 1917. And in that year strange happenings were first reported in the Pension Building.

An elderly guard reported that one night the simulated marble of one of the huge columns began to change its configuration. He swore that he saw the veins slowly shift to form the outline of an Indian, and farther down, a buffalo head. In the morning, the strange profiles were reportedly still there. Then the day guard came in, bringing the morning paper with the news of Bill Cody's death the night before.

That was only the beginning. A few months later someone noticed the outline of a skull in the marble of one of the columns; then other skulls were found in other columns. Some of the guards went so far as to say that one skull in particular seemed to follow them around the great hall. Visitors noticed other strange swirls in the marble. It was said that some of the formations resembled profiles of George and Martha Washington, and what dedicated ghost aficionado would say nay? Newspapers devoted pages, complete with photographs, to the unfolding drama.

More mobile specters have been reported, too. A long time ago, one of the upper floors was used to quarter horses. In more recent years, a watchman reported that one night a rider in a military uniform spurred his mount down a corridor and almost ran him down. Many who thought deeply on this matter were convinced that the night rider was none other than General Meigs, returned to watch over his cathedral.

The strange profiles seem to have faded, but an apparition was reported as recently as 1972, again by a night watchman. He declared he noticed a man in a light-colored suit with a peculiar walk moving toward the great stairway. The watchman followed the man to the third floor, accosted him, and then ran screaming from the building. He told psychiatrists that the man had no eyes, and that he smelled of the stench of the dead.

Who was this disquieting visitor, who had somehow gotten in and out of the building through locked doors? Students of Pension Building lore lean toward James Tanner, one of the first pension administrators, another strong and determined personality. Tanner lost both feet in the second battle of Bull Run, which might explain the odd gait. After his injury, he was retrained as a shorthand clerk, and was pressed into service by Secretary of War Edwin Stanton the night Abraham Lincoln was shot. Tanner transcribed testimony from witnesses at Ford's Theater, scene of the tragedy. He thereafter billed himself as an authority on the assassination and toured the country giving lectures. In fact, he parlayed this notoriety into his appointment as pension commissioner.

Lincoln's son Robert was suspicious of the official version of the assassination. When he was Secretary of War in the 1880s, he approved the plans for the Pension Building, and some believe that he hid secret documents relating to his father's death in one of the hollow columns. Some think that Tanner felt he knew the full story, but never had the proof, and that his spirit roams the big hall in his eternal search for evidence.

What does Elliott think of all this? "I've never seen a ghost," she says, "but my daughter thinks she has. I've certainly not seen any ghosts in the Pension Building; however, I'm not really wild about being here by myself at night."

34
THERE GOES CRAZY HORSE, SITTING BULL WENT THATAWAY, AND CUSTER'S JUST OVER THE HILL

Government agencies are not known for their imagination, but sometimes they surprise you. As described in Chapter 19, the National Park Service takes a lively interest in the paranormal, to the extent of engaging a psychic to calm down the park rangers at the apparently haunted Eisenhower cottage in Gettysburg, Virginia.

And the October 1986 issue of *Courier*, the National Park Service newsletter, devoted three pages to a discussion of a psychic who was engaged to psychometrize relics from the Battle of Little Bighorn. There, in 1876, General George A. Custer's U.S. Army forces met their doom at the hands of Sioux led by Sitting Bull and Crazy Horse.

Psychometry is an ability many psychics have to tell about people and places that have been associated with an object, by holding that object in their hands. I am very cautious about making assured statements about the occult, but I know from personal experience that psychometry works. The first psychic I ever met— knowingly—was a woman named Charlotte Clark, who could do many extraordinary things, and psychometry was one of them. I remember two occasions when she psychometrized objects for me.

I had just discovered the psychic through my new friend Charlotte, and the subject and she were then constituting a large part of my conversation. At a party, a young professor took a lively interest in my friend, and came back with one of his own. He was a devotee of the guru Meher Baba. When I mentioned Charlotte's proficiency at psychometry, he was intrigued and said, "Let's try her out." We went into an adjoining room, and he typed "Meher Baba" on a slip of paper. He gave me his phone number and asked me to call him that night and tell him how Charlotte had done.

When I handed her the slip, Charlotte started to look at what was written on it, then changed her mind, saying she felt she could operate better if her conscious mind was not aware of what she was holding. However, even if she saw the name, I doubt that she would know who Meher Baba was. She read as little as possible about the psychic and spiritual, feeling conscious knowledge of the field might somehow interfere with her powers.

She then told me many things about Meher Baba, things I did not know; I had never heard of him before that afternoon. She described him physically, and mentioned that he often was identified with a grape arbor. She said he had died a few months before, which was true, but was still quite involved with the physical world. Then she began to filter in a description and facts about my new friend, the professor, without differentiating between the guru and the disciple. Things got a little mixed up, but her performance was still impressive. Charlotte was a most adept mind reader, but she told me many things that I did not know about both Meher Baba and my faculty acquaintance, so she could hardly have been reading my mind.

Another time, a friend of mine wanted advice as to whether she should change her job. She knew about Charlotte, although I had never told Charlotte about her. My friend gave me a crucifix she usually wore and asked me to have Charlotte psychometrize it. Charlotte described in detail my friend's appearance, personality, and situation, and she told of a clackety-clack sound around her, which I later found out was an antiquated mimeograph machine she used mornings to copy lesson plans. Charlotte mentioned that around my friend was a very small woman who had a great deal of pain in her feet. This was my friend's mother, whom I knew, but her foot trouble was news to me. So Charlotte could not have been reading my mind about that, either.

I have wandered this far from the hapless Custer and his Indian adversaries to make the point that I have had personal experience with psychometry, and that there seems no question that it can be done.

The psychometrist who reached back in time to that day at Little Bighorn Valley was Howard R. Starkel. Starkel was hired in 1980 by Don Rickey, a former historian at both the U.S. Bureau of Land Management and Custer Battlefield.

Rickey gave Starkel a series of historic objects. Neil C. Mangum, chief historian of the National Park Service, observed the reading.

Starkel explained what he does as follows:

"What I'm doing is focusing my energy flow on the [object]. I have told my people [described as spiritual helpers and guides], 'Let's go.' I shut my eyes and see a sort of screen; but I also become a part of the object in a way. As I go out, projecting to the object, I pick up emotions, then ask [helpers] why the emotion is felt. Vibrations, psychic traces, are left [by human personalities] on objects. [All living things give off and are surrounded by electromagnetic field impulses.] I feel the entity/personality's vibrations inside of me."

For starters, Rickey handed Starkel a very rusted iron spur that was found in the vicinity of the battlefield. It was not an army spur. Starkel was told nothing about it. He took it in his hands, closed his eyes, concentrated for a few seconds, and began speaking:

"I was hurt; this was found in a desolate area. I am with other people. Trees were nearby, in a valley—there is emotion . . . hurry, startled, want to get on horseback, close to a stream, where all my activity was starting, trying to get on horseback. I have been hurt, and want to get across the stream to a hill to defend myself, about 150 yards away from the stream. I want to take off a black boot. I think I was shot and am in pain, but still running. We're just a group, but not the big group. Attackers pulled back. I am crossing the stream with a few others. The larger group is elsewhere. I am a big man, but have no hat. The people chasing me . . . one has a bull's-eye painted on his chest. They are mounted. I feel directionally disoriented. I go across the stream. This spur was lost on the south side just after I crossed the stream to climb the high ridges in a panic to leave. I want to go across the river and north to the main body, but can't. The enemies have backed away; they don't have time to play with us. They go back to fight the main body to the northwest. I see a fire away from the object. Horses are lost at river. The owner did not make it through the battle.''

Rickey pointed out that in the late 1960s, when he was historian at the battlefield, there *were* eroding horse bones on the right side of the Little Bighorn, where General Reno's men had crossed in retreat. Also, Rickey said, the Sioux set fire to the river valley grass during the battle.

In a discussion of the experiment in the *Courier*, Mangum stated that Starkel was not told where the objects originated from or of their usage. Starkel was not familiar with the battlefield. But by psychometrizing the items from the area, he was able to describe the terrain accurately, and was even able to draw maps of it.

Concerning the psychometrizing of the spur as described above, Mangum wrote:

"I was agog. Starkel's words coincided with events of the Reno Valley fight; the valley attack, the river crossing, the bluffs beyond, all formed historically accurate episodes encountered by General Reno's forces in the fight. Futhermore, the scenario fit the description of Dr. James DeWolfe, contract surgeon with Reno's battalion, who was killed on the bluffs after retreating across the Little Bighorn. DeWolf would have been one of the few civilians who could have worn such a spur, as the troopers would have been universally equipped with the military pattern spur.''

Many cartridge shells of different calibers and makes had been gathered for Starkel to read.

"I was stunned," Mangum stated, "by his degree of accuracy. In most instances he came very close to describing where the artifact had been found. One shell selected, a Spencer cartridge, is loaded via a tubular magazine through the butt plate. It was plainly visible to me that Starkel was not familiar with the loading process as he described the insertion of the cartridge in the butt. Starkel stopped in mid-thought, his own curiosity aroused, and asked, 'How could this be?' "

One of the many items Starkel psychometrized was a calvary boot shoe. Portions of his impressions were as follows:

"A helter-skelter situation. . . . It was each for himself; all military discipline had ceased. Wearer was wounded but did not have an instant death. He had more than one wound. He was looking for guidance from someone else. The wearer was confident when in the group, but when isolated from the group he was not a self-motivator. The wearer was part of a smaller group broken off from the main body to go toward the river. The wearer's group rode just to the left of the main body. The main body intended to circle to the northwest, and sweep south down on the Indian camp. Indians were coming up very heavy from the wearer's left. But the initial Indian contact with the main body came from their right front. On the battlefield there was a trough of activity. The wearer swung left to get to a safer area, away from the action, but he was already wounded and was knocked off his horse. But he still had his carbine, and used it. He was crawling; danger was all around. . . . He died in pain, but not in writhing agony. His predominant feeling was 'I don't care.' He was past caring."

Starkel also psychometrized an artifact from the Indian side of the battle, a .50 Martin primed army shell case. Starkel said:

"The user was hostile. He felt very angry, hostile toward the soldiers. He saw them to his east and a little south. They were firing back. No leadership is apparent. There was an attack on them by mounted Indians.

"The shells' user did not lose his life here. He was in another battle somewhere with soldiers. He was experienced. He had not been in the valley very long. He was a nomad, and he fought with a group of comrades. He was a marksman, but the recoil hurt his shoulder. Firing this weapon, there was something like a back blast. He got his shells by stealing, in trade, and so forth.

"I feel his wife had been killed in the recent past, and he blamed the army for this. Several women were killed in a mountainous area, at least one and a half years before this. The group was on the move pretty much ever since. He was a real fighter, an experienced warrior. He enjoyed warfare. He did not know Sitting Bull personally, and he had mixed emotions about him. There was a connection with Crazy Horse, but I don't get it now.

"The shell user walked away when the shooting stopped. The battle was not long, but it was intense. He is looking over his own casualties—scattered. Some scavenging is going on, for weapons and ammunition. An occasional shot is heard. His shoulder is still sore from shooting."

VIII
HEALERS

35
"I'VE SEEN SPIRITS OF THE DEAD—TWICE," SAYS DR. CHRISTIAAN BARNARD

In writing a book of this sort, newspapers and magazines, from the *New York Times* to the *National Enquirer*, are invaluable. But unless all else fails, I use these stories primarily as tips, as starting points. Then the digging begins.

A couple of years ago, the *National Enquirer* published a story on Dr. Christiaan Barnard, the South African surgeon who performed the first heart transplant. The headline: DR. CHRISTIAAN BARNARD: I'VE SEEN SPIRITS OF THE DEAD—TWICE.

According to the *National Enquirer*, Barnard made the statement about seeing apparitions on an Italian TV show, "Mr. O," which is watched by millions of viewers. He said he had his first encounter with a spirit eighteen years earlier, when he was in a hospital recovering from hepatitis. About 10 P.M. a woman entered his private room.

Dr. Christiaan Barnard

"She walked toward my bed," he said, "put her hand on my chest and began pushing against it. I looked up at her and saw she was very thin and pale, with blue eyes and gray hair. I took her wrists in my hand. They were very fragile. I pushed her back and realized she was extremely light. Then, as if she were reacting to my pressure, she levitated and disappeared through the window."

He rang for a nurse; when she arrived she apologized for the delay, saying a woman had just died on her ward. When Barnard asked her to describe the woman it was obvious it was the same person he had seen.

"I had seen the spirit of this woman who had just died," he said.

His other experience with a spirit came just after the sudden death of his father.

"I was living in Cape Town, and he lived about 300

miles away," Barnard said. "By the time I arrived, he had already died. That night I was lying in bed feeling very sad. I was in tears. Suddenly I felt someone touch my shoulder. I turned and saw my father next to me. He did not smile, but was content and calm.

"He told me, 'Don't be sad. I'm not dead. I don't live anymore in this world. I belong to another world now. But don't be sad, because there is nothing bad in my new way of being.' And then he disappeared. Both these experiences were so real that I can believe there is certainly something beyond life."

When I phoned the Transplantation Institute of the Baptist Medical Center in Oklahoma City, where Barnard was working, I spoke with a staff member who said Barnard was in a meeting. I told her I wanted to know about Barnard's encounters with the dead; she said she'd ask him when he was available and would get back to me.

The next day she called and said, "He chuckled and said, 'I'd forgotten all about that. I really don't want to talk about it anymore.' "

"Well," I said, "it apparently was true, then."

"He said he'd forgotten about it, so I guess it was," she replied.

36
CARL GUSTAV JUNG—
SCIENTIST AND MYSTIC

C arl Gustav Jung, the Swiss psychiatrist and
founder of analytical psychology, was distinguished for his investigations of the unconscious and mythology. From his youth, he was aware of
the occult. Psychic events happened around him and to
him. In fact, occasionally he seemed to have caused
them.

One of his best-known encounters was with Sig-
mund Freud. Early in his career, Jung was a disciple of
the founder of psychoanalysis, but later broke with
him. For one thing, Jung differed with Freud's insis-
tence on the sexual basis of neurosis. As time went on,
Jung began to see his mentor as something of a know-
it-all, unwilling to give credence to the ideas of others.
Jung, a powerful and self-willed personality, was not
likely to remain permanently in a subordinate position.

Things might have been coming to a head when the following strange incident occurred in 1909. Jung was eager to hear Freud's views on precognition and parapsychology. Freud summarily rejected the entire subject, although some years later he did an about-face and acknowledged the factuality of occult phenomena. Jung was obviously coming to a boil. He wrote in his book *Memories, Dreams, Reflections*:

"While Freud was going on this way, I had a curious sensation. It was as if my diaphragm were made of iron and were becoming red-hot—a glowing vault. And at that moment there was such a loud report in the bookcase, which stood right next to us, that we both started up in alarm, fearing the thing was going to topple over on us. I said to Freud, 'There, that is an example of a so-called catalytic exteriorization phenomenon.'

" 'Oh, come,' he said, 'that is sheer bosh!'

" 'It is not,' I replied. 'You are mistaken, Herr Professor. And to prove my point I now predict that in a moment there will be another such loud report!' Sure enough, no sooner had I said the words than the same detonation went off in the bookcase.

"To this day I do not know what gave me this certainty. But I knew beyond all doubt that the report would come again. Freud only stared aghast at me. I do not know what was in his mind, or what his look meant. In any case, this incident aroused his mistrust of me, and I had the feeling that I had done something against him. I never afterwards discussed the incident with him."

A similar happening had occurred much earlier, when Jung was still in college. He wrote:

"One day I was sitting in my room, studying my

textbooks. In the adjoining room, the door to which stood ajar, my mother was knitting. That was our dining room, where the round walnut dining table stood. The table had come from the dowry of my paternal grandmother, and was at this time about seventy years old. My mother was sitting by the window, about a yard away from the table. . . . Suddenly there sounded a report like a pistol shot. I jumped up and rushed into the room from which the noise of the explosion had come. My mother was sitting flabbergasted in her armchair, the knitting fallen from her hand. She stammered out, 'W-w-what's happened? It was right beside me!' and stared at the table. Following her eyes, I saw what had happened. The table top had split from the rim to beyond the center, and not along any joint; the split ran right through the solid wood. I was thunderstruck. How could such a thing happen? A table of solid walnut that had dried out for seventy years—how could it split on a summer day in the relatively high degree of humidity characteristic of our climate? If it had stood next to a heated stove on a cold, dry winter day, then it might have been conceivable. . . .

"Some two weeks later, I came home at six o'clock in the evening and found the household—my mother, my fourteen-year-old sister, and the maid—in a great state of agitation. About an hour earlier there had been another deafening report. This time it was not the already damaged table; the noise had come from the direction of the sideboard, a heavy piece of furniture dating from the early nineteenth century. They had already looked all over it, but had found no traces of a split. I immediately began examining the sideboard and the entire surrounding area, but just as fruitlessly.

Then I began on the interior of the sideboard. In the cupboard containing the bread basket I found a loaf of bread, and, beside it, the bread knife. The greater part of the blade had been snapped off in several pieces. The handle lay in one corner of the rectangular basket, and in each of the other corners a piece of the blade. . . .

"The next day I took the shattered knife to one of the best cutlers in the town. He examined the fractures with a magnifying glass, and shook his head. 'This knife is perfectly sound,' he said. 'There is no fault in the steel. Someone must have deliberately broken it piece by piece.' "

A few weeks later Jung heard that some of his relatives had been engaged in séances with a medium, a teenage girl who produced somnambulistic states and spiritualistic phenomena. He wondered if the strange occurrences in his house might have some connection with this medium. He began attending regular séances and observed tapping noises from the walls and the table. The girl, of little education, saw visions and received mediumistic communications. While in such states she spoke stilted high German instead of her accustomed Swiss dialect. Jung's notes on the girl and the séances formed an important part of his doctoral thesis.

An extraordinary haunting experience happened to Jung in 1920, when he spent several weekends in a country house a friend had rented. During the night he experienced several increasingly haunting phenomena such as knocking, disagreeable odors, rustling, and sounds of dripping water. The incidents climaxed with the appearance, or vision, of an old woman's head on the pillow about two feet away from him. Actually, it was one half of a face. The eye seemed to be wide open and glared at him. Then the head disappeared. Jung reported that he lit a candle and spent the rest of the night sitting in a chair. He and his friend found out later that the house was known to be haunted and that sooner or later all tenants were frightened away.

For a time in 1916, a series of parapsychological events happened in Jung's home. Blankets were suddenly snatched away. One of his daughters saw a white figure passing through her room. The strange happenings culminated one Sunday afternoon when the whole family and two maids heard the front door bell ringing frantically. Jung not only heard it but saw the bell moving. But, although they investigated while the bell was still ringing, no one was at the door.

Everyone in the house felt an impossibly thick atmosphere. Jung dealt with his emotions by going to his study and letting his unconscious express itself in a document he called "Septem Sermones ad Mortuos." He said, "As soon as I took up the pen, the whole ghostly assemblage evaporated. The room quieted and the atmosphere cleared. The haunting was over."

Barbara Hannah, a Jungian analyst, wrote in her book, *Jung: His Life and Work*:

"This was, I believe, the first time he experienced the fact that such parapsychological phenomena often take place when there is something in the unconscious that is striving to become conscious. Later, Jung often experienced such phenomena [loud reports in the furniture, for example] as a pre-stage to a creative effort [usually they occurred *before* he realized what he was going to write]. This is also probably the reason why parapsychological phenomena [in the form of poltergeists] are particularly frequent in the neighborhood of adolescents who have not yet become conscious of the great change that is taking place in them. One wonders whether the particularly violent phenomena [table and knife] during his time as an undergraduate had anything to do with the fact that he was not yet conscious of his destiny as a psychiatrist and 'an explorer of the human soul and its hidden depths.' "

Throughout his life, Jung had experiences with what seemed to be spirits. He wrote in *Memories, Dreams, Reflections*:

"One night I lay awake thinking of the sudden death of a friend whose funeral had taken place the day before. I was deeply concerned. Suddenly I felt he was in the room. It seemed to me that he stood at the foot of my bed and was asking me to go with him. I did not have the feeling of an apparition; rather, it was an inner visual image of him, which I explained to myself as a fantasy."

Jung went on to say he decided, "I might as well give him the benefit of the doubt and for experiment's sake credit him with reality." He wrote:

"The moment I had that thought, he went to the door and beckoned me to follow him. So I was going to have to play along with him! He led me out of the house, into the garden, out to the road, and finally to his house. In reality it was several hundred yards away from mine. I went in, and he conducted me into his study. He climbed on a stool and showed me the second of five books with red bindings which stood on the second shelf from the top. Then the vision broke off. I was not acquainted with his library and did not know what books he owned. Certainly I could never have made out from below the titles of the books he had pointed out to me on the second shelf from the top.

"This experience seemed to me so curious that next morning I went to his widow and asked whether I could look up something in my friend's library. Sure enough, there was a stool standing under the bookcase I had seen in my vision, and even before I came closer I could see the five books with red bindings. I stepped up on the stool so as to be able to read the titles. They were translations of the novels of Emile Zola. The title of the second volume read: *The Legacy of the Dead.*"

A perusal of writings by or about Jung turns up passage after passage relating to the paranormal. For example, in his preface to a book by a colleague, Aniela Jaffe, called *Apparitions and Precognition*, Jung wrote:

"I know from my own experience, and that of other investigators, magic as practiced in the Middle Ages and much remoter times has by no means died out, but still flourishes. The life of the centuries lives on, and things that have accompanied human life from time immemorial continue to happen: premonitions, foreknowledge, second sight, hauntings, ghosts, return of the dead, bewitchings, sorcery, magic spells. One doesn't speak of these things, however. They simply happen, and the intellectuals know nothing of them— for intellectuals know neither themselves nor people as they really are."

37
NORMAN VINCENT PEALE AND HIS MYSTICAL EXPERIENCES

The concept of ghosts—the word itself, per-haps—is often frightening to the convention-ally religious person. Ghosts do not fit into the dogmas of most theologies. Mysticism and piety are somewhat different. A case in point is Norman Vincent Peale.

As I proceeded on this book it struck me that I was writing a great deal about colorful eccentrics—actors, musicians, writers, and characters of that ilk. Why shouldn't they see, or be, ghosts? After all, they're pretty strange, alive or dead. It occurred to me that I ought to start getting a few solid citizens into this book—busi-nessmen, military men, engineers, Republicans. Then I heard that Norman Vincent Peale has written in his autobiography about seeing, or being aware of in some way, his deceased mother, father, and brother. The very man, I thought; no one could be more respectable than Norman Vincent Peale.

So I decided to check him out and, if possible, interview him. It had been some forty years since I had had traffic with the Reverend Peale. He is best known, of course, for his bonanza bestseller *The Power of Positive Thinking*. But for many years he wrote a newspaper column. I read it regularly as a youth. I was paid to. In fact, required to. Early in my newspaper career I was shanghaied onto a copy desk in Rochester, New York. The paper ran Peale's column, and since I was the most junior on the desk, it became my duty to read Peale's copy and write a headline. It was a job that the raunchy sophisticates of the rim gleefully dumped on me. Eventually, I went on to other, if not greater, things and Norman Vincent Peale faded almost completely from my consciousness.

And so, forty years later, I wrote to Peale's publisher for assistance in my current project. Nothing seemed to be happening, so I called Peale's organization, Foundation for Christian Living, in Pawling, New York. When I spoke to his secretary, explaining I had heard that her employer had had psychic experiences, the word *psychic* seemed to send mild shock waves through the lady. I asked what she would call them, and she offered the term *spiritual*.

"Okay," I replied, "spiritual—it's just semantics."

At any rate, within a couple of days I received in the mail his autobiography, *The True Joy of Positive Living*. With it was a short letter from Peale himself. He objected to my alluding in my letter to his publisher to his having "seen apparitions." But he had, he said, had "experiences in the realm of departed loved ones," and he referred me to Chapter 21.

Peale's Chapter 21 is of definite interest to people

reading about ghosts, since he claims to have seen three of them. I have to hand it to him for going out on a limb, no matter what he calls them. Peale puts the subject at the very end of his book, and leads into it gingerly, but bravely, considering his audience:

"There is [an] area which we, like primitive man, think of as miraculous or outside natural law. And in referring to it, we use such terms as 'mysterious,' 'physical,' 'extrasensory perception,' or 'beyond sense.' We even call it clairvoyance or, at its worst, phony. People who dabble in it are in danger of being considered oddballs or dreamy-eyed. But along have come a few adventurers in thinking like Steinmetz, Edison, Einstein, McDougal, Rhine, and others, notable scientific scholars who lend credibility to a vast body of truth that obviously exists but remains practically unexplored."

Peale then gave as an example the electric fan. When it is not turned on, one cannot see through the blades; when it is turned up to high speed, one can see through it clearly.

"In similar fashion," he wrote, "though in a much more sophisticated way, the higher elevation of spiritual insights may now and then penetrate the barrier between this side and the other and provide glimpses or intuition or some sort of perceptions or flashing illuminations of that heaven which does more truly than ever imagined lie beyond. And it is to this superimposed state of life, this heaven, that our deceased loved ones have gone and to which we, in our time, shall pass through a gate we call death but which more accurately is the entrance to a higher life."

Peale went on to tell of the death of his mother. "One

night my mother died after a joyful evening we had spent together in the family home. . . . Distraught, I went to my study in the church, the windows of which face Fifth Avenue." He told of putting his hands on a Bible his mother had given him.

"Suddenly," he wrote, "I seem to feel two cupped hands resting lightly but distinctly upon my head. . . . I heard no voice. I saw nothing. I only felt the hands, and unmistakably they were her own, comforting me. Alone in my sorrow and reaching out, did I attain for one fleeting second the higher frequency, and did she, reaching back, cause mother and son to make a quick but unmistakable contact between time and eternity."

Some years later, Peale bought an expensive hurricane lamp for his wife, and felt concerned about spending so much money. Soon after, he wrote, he had another mystical experience in the parking lot of a Howard Johnson's.

"Mother's presence suddenly seemed to materialize and said to me distinctly: 'Stop worrying about those hurricane lamps. Ruth is a wonderful girl. Nothing is too good for her.' And then she was gone."

Later, he describes being on the platform in a large auditorium with an important bishop. Some ten thousand people were present. "Then," he wrote, "I 'saw' him, my father who had died long before at age eighty-five. He came striding down the aisle, singing. He appeared to be about forty years old, in the prime of life, no more arthritis, no sign of stroke or enfeebled body. He was vigorous and obviously happy, and gave every evidence of enjoying life.

"I was spellbound, completely lost in what I was 'seeing.' The huge audience faded away. I was only

with him. Getting closer, he smiled that great old smile
of his and raised his arm in the old-time familiar
gesture as he moved strongly forward on spritely step. I
arose from the chair, advanced to the edge of the platform, reaching for him. Then he was gone, leaving me
shaken, somewhat embarrassed by my actions, but
happy at the same time."

He described visiting one of his boyhood homes, not
long after, again in the presence of an important person, the publisher of the *Cincinnati Enquirer*. Suddenly, he wrote, a "profound mystical experience and
vision occurred. It seemed that I was removed from
worldly reality and was once again a small boy standing on that sidewalk, holding the hand of my little
brother Bob. The two of us were dressed up as children
were in those days. We were waiting for Mother and
Father. Then the door opened, and they came down the
steps. Mother was wearing an old-fashioned dress that
reached her shoetops. The dress seemed to be made of a
lacelike material with a full skirt and a narrow waist,
and a high collar giving a choker effect. Her hair was
piled high and a hat added grace and charm. She
seemed about thirty-five years of age. Father appeared
to be about forty and was dressed in a suit of a dark blue
serge, a derby hat atop his head. He took mother's arm,
and with his accustomed vigor and old-style courtesy,
was escorting her down the steps. They were smiling at
us. The experience was so completely real and I was so
lost in it that I started to rush toward them. That broke
the spell and the vision vanished. But the reality to me
was unmistakable."

Finally, Peale told of his brother, a surgeon, who had
died only a few weeks before. Peale was speaking at a

prayer meeting of employees of his organization. He wrote:

"This day while I was speaking, suddenly I no longer saw the audience, I only 'saw' my brother Bob. . . . Bob was striding . . . vigorously and full of life. He was young and zestful, exuding joy and enthusiasm. He, too, had his arm raised in a gesture characteristic of him, and his old charming smile was evident. He seemed to say, 'It's O.K., Deacon,' using a nickname only he had ever applied to me, 'it's O.K.' Then he vanished.

"However, this strange happening served to deepen my conviction about four facts: (1) Our loved ones who 'have died in the Lord' are not dead; (2) they live and grow and are well and happy; (3) their love for us continues; (4) they are near. And though they live in another and higher dimension, at rare times they may break through the barrier. But if they do not reach you as others have been reached by their loved ones, the relationships continue to exist, awaiting your acceptance of them."

IX

RETURN VIA TAPE RECORDER

38
VOICES OF THE DEAD ON TAPE? ANWAR SADAT, BENJAMIN FRANKLIN, CARL JUNG, ADOLF HITLER

On the morning of October 7, 1981, Sarah Estep was taping in her home near Baltimore. She did this every morning, turning on her tape recorder for about ten minutes. She was alone and was not speaking. She was expecting messages from the dead.

Estep had become interested in the phenomenon of taped voices several years before and had taped hundreds of voices from out of the blue. She had, in fact, formed the American Association–Electronic Voice Phenomena for people interested in recording such voices.

She had heard on the radio that morning that Anwar Sadat, the Egyptian president, had been shot but was not in serious condition. But in her taping session later that morning, she told me, the first thing that came through was a message, "May the God give off . . . may

293

the God give off . . ." A few seconds later, the voice said, "God the giver, God the giver."

She told me she felt immediately that this was Sadat, and that he had died. She knew his voice from hearing it on TV.

Estep is a down-to-earth sort of woman, well-educated and cautious in her conclusions. She has been a school teacher, a social worker, and a camp director. She avoids dogmatic statements; she is not absolutely sure that was Sadat, but she suspects it was.

In her ten years of taping, she recorded thousands of voices, and a few have purported to be those of famous people.

"About six years ago," she says, "I was doing my regular morning taping and someone said, 'This is Ben,' and shortly after, 'This is Franklin.' I asked if I had Benjamin Franklin with me. About half an hour later a very loud, shrill voice, filled with emotion, came through and shrieked, 'He's still on earth!' Benjamin Franklin was a firm believer in reincarnation, and whether that meant he is reincarnated and back on Earth I don't know. One of my ancestors, James Wilson, was a very good friend of Ben Franklin's. In fact, they started the University of Pennsylvania Law School together. Whether someone on the other side picked this up, I don't know. What we can make of it, I'm not sure."

Estep's messages are among literally millions of communications that seem to have been received via tape recorder in the past thirty or more years. The technique is easy; one simply lets a tape recorder run in a quiet room and then plays it back. Sometimes there will be voices on the tape—usually short messages, a half-dozen words or less, although sometimes messages of more than a dozen words are recorded. Either a reel-to-reel or a cassette recorder will work.

Messages have reportedly been received ever since recording devices have been in existence. In fact, it is said that when Thomas Edison invented the phonograph he was searching for a means of recording voices of the dead. Some researchers, such as the Californian Attila von Szalay, are reported to have noted the phenomenon in the mid-1950s. However, the first person to publicize taped voices widely was Friedrich Jurgenson, who was well known in Sweden as a painter, opera singer, and film producer.

In the spring of 1959, Jurgenson went into the fields near his country home to record bird calls. When he played the tape he was startled to hear a masculine voice discussing bird calls in Norwegian. At first he thought he might in some way have picked up a stray radio signal, but as he continued taping he began to get messages from people he knew who had died. Sometimes they addressed him by name. One message was from his mother, saying, "Friedel, my little Friedel, can you hear me?"

Jurgenson wrote a book about his experiences, and began to receive many visitors who had also heard taped voices. One reported a male voice saying, "I am living!" Another voice, sounding like that of a young woman, said, "They can hear us on Earth."

One of Jurgenson's most significant readers was a Latvian-born scholar living in Sweden named Konstantin Raudive, who was so impressed by Jurgenson's accounts that he devoted the remainder of his life to recording and studying taped voices. In ten years, he reported, he recorded some one hundred thousand of them; since he spoke seven languages he was well-equipped for the task. He became so identified with the phenomenon that for a time the voices were known as the Raudive voices.

In the late 1960s, Raudive published a book in German called *Unhorbares Wird Horbar,* literally translated as *The Inaudible Becomes Audible.* It was published in the United States in 1971 under the title *Breakthrough.* A typical scholar's tome, the book is ponderously written, which might have some bearing on why it did not receive more attention. A more likely explanation is the reluctance of the human mind to relinquish fixed notions—in this case, the impossibility of communication between the living and the dead.

In any case, Raudive purports to record messages from or about such famous people as Leo Tolstoy, Maxim Gorky, Freidrich Nietzsche, Carl Jung, John F. Kennedy, Winston Churchill, Joseph Stalin, Adolf Hitler, Benito Mussolini, and others. The messages, similar to scores of messages in the book from lesser known spirits, are fragmentary, half a dozen words or less.

Death doesn't seem to change people much. Raudive wrote: "The German dictator Adolf Hitler manifests most frequently and one gains the impression that even in the transcendental dimension he now inhabits, he shows exactly the same traits that characterized him on Earth: self-glorification, persistence in pushing himself forward, and a certain spiritual depravity." Many of the entities who speak of Hitler deplore him, but Raudive adds that he still has his followers on the other side.

Peter Bander, editor of the version of Raudive's book that was published in England, wrote a preface to the English edition, and has also written a book of his own, *Voice From the Tapes*. He related that his partner, Colin Smythe, had been approached at the Frankfort Book Fair and presented with Raudive's book, in its German incarnation. Both Smythe and Bander, the latter of whom is a psychologist and a theologian, were wary of Raudive's claims. However, Bander was favorably inclined by something Smythe had done and then told Bander only after the fact. Smythe had bought some recording tapes and let them run. On one of them there seemed to be a voice, but Smythe could not make it out and asked Bander to listen to the tape. When Bander did, he said he heard the voice of his mother saying in German, *"Mach die Tur mal auf"*—or "Why don't you open the door?"

They began to think seriously about publishing Raudive's book. However, Sir Robert Mayer, chairman of the firm, still had reservations. It was decided to arrange a further test, at which Raudive himself would be present. Top-notch electronics technicians were engaged, and a number of distinguished people were invited. Bander wrote:

"Raudive invited all of us to state our names and, if we wanted to, to ask any of our departed friends to communicate. Mayer took this opportunity. 'I am ninety-two years old,' he said, 'and most of my contemporaries are dead. Would it not be reasonable to assume that I, or my wife, for that matter, should be getting far more messages tonight than anybody here? One of our dearest friends, the late Artur Schnabel, would never miss such an opportunity of getting in touch.' "

Voices proliferated on the tapes over the next few hours, and some were purportedly from Schnabel, the famed concert pianist. They were brief and fragmentary, in German, such as, *"Artur, wir sind hier,"* meaning "Artur, we are here." At one point there was a long sentence in which only two words were intelligible: "Artur" and "Barbirolli." Sir John Barbirolli, a famed orchestra conductor who had just died, was a close friend of the Mayers.

Bander wrote: "After a first examination that lasted about two hours, we had identified over two hundred places where voices were discernable. Twenty-seven voices were so clear that Ken Attwood (one of the engineers) suggested a powerful loudspeaker might be connected to the tape recorder instead of the earphones, so that everybody could listen."

Mayer's reaction at the end of the evening was brief and to the point. "Peter," he said, "we publish!" Speaking to a newspaperman who was present, he said, "After ninety-two years it looks as if I have to adjust myself to some form of activity after I have left this Earth." Lady Mayer said the demonstration was "only confirmation of what I have believed and known for a long time. However, this material proof is exciting and challenging, and the churches should take up the challenge science provides them with."

In this book, of course, we are primarily concerned with shades of the rich and/or famous, and Bander has this to say:

"The voices of the famous or infamous which Raudive purports to have recorded have presented me with more difficulties. . . . I cannot help feeling that name-dropping, a very human weakness, has either entered the celestial realms or is being projected into them by Raudive. In fairness to Raudive, I must say that it has been pointed out to me on several occasions that it was not unreasonable for those voices to dominate, as the purported originators during their lifetimes on Earth were equally vociferous."

Bander also commented: "The vast majority of the voices I have heard during the many tests and experiments carried out in my presence seemed to come from persons who had a strong link with one or more of the experimenters. This can be explained far more easily than voices purporting to come from statesmen, famous authors, and philosophers, with perhaps one notable exception, Carl Gustav Jung, the psychologist."

Bander seemed to feel that Jung had something significant to say. I turned eagerly to the pages in *Breakthrough* where Jung is noted, bracketed by such other heavy hitters as Nietzsche, Ortega y Gasset, and Sir Oliver Lodge. I was somewhat disappointed and rather mystified as to what had so impressed Bander. The most intriguing Jungian quotes I could find were as follows:

"Now fashions are terribly vain." "We are here, good day." "You belong probably to the cucumbers."

Raudive commented on the last: "The meaning of 'cucumbers' seems obscure."

This took me back some thirty years to my only experience with table tipping, when I received the cryptic but unforgettable communication, "Throw putty deep in the ocean cool."

Concerning Bander's suspicion that Raudive might have been projecting the messages onto the tape himself, it is true that there is solid evidence that living people can sometimes put their thoughts onto tape, so there is the inevitable question: How dead are the voices? But there have been many cases in which the taped voices were in languages not understood by anyone involved in the taping, or, so far as anyone knew, in the vicinity. Estep, who now numbers some three hundred active members in forty-one states and eleven foreign countries in her taped voices organization, put it this way to me:

"I'm a person who likes things in black and white," she said, merrily mixing her metaphors, "and this is why I like the electronic voice. I don't dismiss mediumistic communication, but it can be very difficult to tell what is genuine and what isn't. Many people who feel they're in contact with the unseen are just deluded. One doesn't really know. But the tape voices are objective. They are there, and they can be played over and over."

X

WHAT IS THIS THING CALLED CHANNELING?

39
CELEBRITIES GALORE—
THEY'RE POURING DOWN
THROUGH THE
CHANNELERS!

What is this thing called channeling? To many a current searcher, it's what psychoanalysis, group therapy, LSD, EST, yoga, grass, and nude hot-tubbing were in decades not long gone.

It seems to be a sort of do-it-yourself mediumship. It's a good bet that someone on your block is channeling. They are—or think they are, or pretend they are— receiving messages from an other-worldly source. This source could be anything from Cousin Maude who drank herself to death in the fifties to a Hindu god-man who goes back thirty-five thousand years, from an extraterrestial entity to a group of spirits who may or may not have ever incarnated on Earth.

Channeling is up for grabs. I know a woman who puts out a monthly newsletter incorporating the inspirations she receives while channeling. I think the lady is channeling her unconscious—it's hard to believe any spirit could deliver such banalities. Although on second thought, why not? They say one doesn't change instantly when one dies. Once a bore, always a bore. At least for a millenium or two.

I asked a friend of mine, Roger Pile of Ivoryton, Connecticut, an accomplished medium, to define the term. He offered this: *"Channeling* has become a buzz word because it's a more comfortable word than *mediumship*, so the term has gotten to be popular. It's an acceptable word. Somehow mediums are mysterious and special, but a channeler—anybody can do it. It's become a chic thing."

Anne Gehman, a highly regarded medium, says: "I do believe that a lot of the channeling is valid. The general public has evolved to a certain consciousness and interest in the other world. I think people are hungering for spiritual knowledge. But I think that a lot of it that has been promoted is very commercial and has not been particularly valid or good.

"I think some people get a shiver or a shake or feel a slight breeze, and immediately they think they're unfolded or developed, and they're ready to serve. But a lot of what is coming through is colored by their own thinking a great deal. I think a lot of the so-called channelers are saying what *they* want to say. Because they don't have the courage to say it, they're attributing it to spirit."

Concerning channelers or mediums such as the ones in this chapter Gehman says, "It just seems to me unlikely that one person is going to connect with all these famous people."

The research for this book would have been simpler if I had just gone to a few of the more publicized

(Doonesbury cartoon—channeling)

exponents of channeling, the ones who specialize in bringing through famous people. Obviously, I am not unwilling to entertain the possibility of visits from the greats of yesteryear; otherwise, writing this book would have been an utterly cynical undertaking. The preceding chapters are shot through with mediums and psychics who give accounts of contacts with famous shades—but they don't make a habit, or even a cottage industry, of it. I take them seriously; I have a strong feeling that they are doing what they say they are doing.

But there are some psychics about whom I feel a nagging urge do some extended thinking. Their claims produce in me a mind-set that was well-expressed by the late parapsychologist J. Gaither Pratt: "Be bold to look, but cautious to conclude."

I shrink from being rudely skeptical. P. T. Barnum has been quoted: "More persons, on the whole, are humbugged by believing nothing than by believing too much." On the other hand, who wants to be taken for a ride? Yet, could one be doing an injustice by such incredulity? Let us at least consider some psychics who constantly, they tell us, deal with departed celebrities.

Elwood Babbitt is a medium who lives in rural Massachusetts. In its June/July/August 1983 issue, *Psychic Guide* featured a striking caricature of Samuel Clemens/Mark Twain on its cover. Inside was an extensive interview, through Babbitt, of Clemens. The interview was conducted by the magazine's editor, Paul Zuromski. In an accompanying box, Frangcon Jones, an English professor at Keene (New Hampshire) State University, says he thinks it really is Clemens who is coming through, that a number of reasonably esoteric questions involving events of his life are answered correctly.

I called a man who won a Pulitzer Prize for a biography of Mark Twain. Justin Kaplan is a former professor at Harvard University; his book is *Mr. Clemens and Mark Twain.* I sent him a copy of the *Psychic Guide* interview and asked him what he thought of it.

"It was entertaining, and a wonderful piece of vaudeville," he said.

But did you think it sounded like Mark Twain? I asked.

"It sounded like bullshit to me," he said. "A real old stager. It sounded like a Mark Twain actor. It doesn't sound like Mark Twain, it sounds like pure horseshit. But it's entertaining, if he's not trying to kid anyone."

Ah, I interposed, but Babbitt *is* claiming this is the real Mark Twain.

"Well," Kaplan replied, "the only thing he may have in common with Mark Twain is his joy in fooling people. If people are fools enough to believe him, that's the funniest part of the joke."

That's laying it on the line, but I think that in all fairness I should mention I don't think Kaplan believed in ghosts to start with.

It's true that the interview is clever. But is it really Twain, or is it pure Babbittry? (*Psychic Guide* sells tapes and books on Babbitt channeling such luminaries as Mohandas Gandhi, Albert Einstein, Winston Churchill, Martin Luther King, Abraham Lincoln, John F. Kennedy, and Bishop Pike. We are offered eighteen talks with Jesus, four with St. Luke, four with Jesus's teachers, and one with Jesus's father.)

It's interesting to note that when I called Babbitt

Elwood Babbitt

while doing preliminary research, he was quite rude
and refused to talk, which startled me because he had
heretofore been friendly and helpful. Maybe, being a
psychic, he had an inkling that I was going to clobber
him long before I knew it.

It is true that Babbitt's version of Twain is amusing
and entertaining. Here is the way it starts:

CLEMENS: "Yes, I'm Sam Clemens. And I'm glad
to have kept you waiting. Namely because the
great architect decided that we all wear gas
masks in order to enter the atmosphere of Earth
once again."

Later, he goes on:

CLEMENS: If I might say so, in the hardened conditions of the intellect I see on earth, if Jesus
Christ walked down the street of your capital, or
walked into one of your churches, and he an-

nounced himself with great manifestations of healing and prophecy, no one would believe him.

ZUROMSKI: Have you seen Jesus?

CLEMENS: I've talked with him, and he's an ordinary fellow like you. He is very compassionate, but very misunderstood by his PR men as we'll call them. . . . He is genuine and you will find that he is one of the greatest mediums, as you call it, of the day, but no one wants to admit it.

ZUROMSKI: How's life on the other side?

CLEMENS: I am able to float along with high velocity, which I enjoy, to any specific place I want. I also go to various schools.

I enjoy my "Cloud 9." I have all the ladies I like to enjoy and orgasmic experiences that do not require the intimacy of coitus as in the physical body. I just merge with these dewdrops of energies of ladies and men creating the oneness which life is all about.

(John Lennon supposedly reports something similar, another footnote to the ongoing debate: Is there sex after death? It should be safe, at least.)

Another "Clemens" quote:

CLEMENS: Let us understand that politicians are not born, they are excreted.

ZUROMSKI: What do you think of Ronald Reagan?

CLEMENS: The president of your United States, tragically enough, was an actor. He should continue to be one because he is only a pretender in his desire to exclude the poor and shape your democracy into more of a dictatorship. I think he would make an excellent cowboy, a bullrider, or matador. That is where his greater talents lie . . . on his rump.

On a different subject:

CLEMENS: You have the motor car in your world. We've always spoken about Yankee ingenuity, but you mean to tell me that America and its workers cannot manufacture a standard car that can last twenty years? And not practice at the greed that puts the obsolescence planned into any vehicle made? People are being bilked by car manufacturers.

Zuromski asked how Clemens liked Hartford, where he lived for a time.

CLEMENS: Horrendous! The whole world is horrendous! If you could view it from other galaxies, the steam and stench that comes from your planet is heinous.

Well, Hal Holbrook couldn't have done it better— nor, for all we know—could Mark Twain.

Dr. Robert R. Leichtman came to Baltimore in the mid-seventies, partly because he was attracted to the East Coast, which he considers a more cultured area than his native Midwest, and partly because he wanted to work with the late Olga Worrell, the famed spiritual healer. He is still very much involved with spiritual healing.

Dr. Robert Leichtman   *(Photo by Leonard L. Greif, Jr.)*

He has, he wrote me, "published twenty-four books of interviews with 'famous' spirits." I've spoken at length with him on the phone, and he is a highly educated professional man. He is a graduate of the University of Iowa Medical School and gives the impression of being something of a scholar, which may or may not be in his favor in this particular inquiry.

Leichtman told me that he is a medium and that he began to be aware of his psychic abilities in the sixties.

For his books, he sometimes uses two or three other mediums as well as himself. He said he made his first contact with a famous person in the late sixties: Madame H. P. Blavatsky, founder of Theosophy.

I mentioned that I had written a chapter in which a number of people had claimed to have channeled John Lennon. He was not impressed with Lennon. "Lennon was really not a very evolved person," he said. "He really was not much more than a kind of thug from England. I can't imagine that he had that much worthwhile to say."

I mentioned that Lennon had become very much involved with the spiritual before he died, that he had in fact undergone what seemed a marked personality development. I don't know if Leichtman gave that any credence, but I wouldn't bet on Lennon's showing up in any of his books.

I asked Leichtman how he knew these were the real spirits of famed people he was dealing with.

First, he said, he has worked with some spirits whose integrity he is confident of for many years and these spirits investigate entities claiming to be famous people, to sift out any imposters.

"Second," Leichtman said, "you expect to have an intelligent conversation, something that is meaningful, something that indicates this person has an intelligence and understanding equivalent to or greater than the personality. Someone who is familiar with the intricacies of the area that dominated that personality during physical life. They should sound like they could be that person. Sometimes there is a spirit that claims to be Thomas Jefferson but sounds like some left-wing political nut, not like Jefferson at all."

"The third quality is a presence that often comes with these people. For instance, Rembrandt has a very intense love and dedication that came with him. You knew you were in the presence of a very spiritual person. Then there are their dominant elements of personality. For example, Roosevelt loved to talk and talk and talk. He loved to go on about all sorts of things, thoroughly enjoying himself.

"Freud was very reticent, very quiet, very meticulous in his statements, very thoughtful of what he was saying. He was that sort of reserved, cautious individual that he was in life.

"Franklin was every inch the diplomat. We had a hard time getting him to answer our questions if he didn't want to answer. He waltzes all around the area when he wants to avoid a direct answer. He was obviously a very humorous person, very friendly, very amiable, as I guess he was in real life."

I asked a highly respected medium who has met Leichtman and has read some of his book what she thought. She asked to remain anonymous. This is what she said: "Some of what I read didn't carry with it the loftiness that I would expect from a more evolved spirit. The terminology is even all the same. The people speak exactly alike, using the same vocabulary. Those personalites do not come through in that writing."

Speaking with caution—I could be mistaken—I felt the same way when I read Leichtman's books.

Leichtman's publisher, Ariel Press of 4082 Clotts Road, Columbus, Ohio, sent me a dozen of his paperbacks of about one-hundred pages each—*Shakespeare Returns, Mark Twain Returns, Lincoln Returns, Jung &*

Freud Return, Burbank Returns, Jefferson Returns, Nikola Tesla Returns, Churchill Returns, Franklin Returns, Schweitzer Returns, and *Einstein Returns.* He also wrote *The Destiny of America,* in which Alexander Hamilton, Thomas Jefferson, Benjamin Franklin, Franklin D. Roosevelt, and George Washington return.

A lot of what I was reading sounded very much like Leichtman, not like the personalities in question.

For example, I had always thought that Thomas Jefferson was a voice of liberalism, but Leichtman has him saying, in 1984, the day of Reaganomics: "The current administration is a breath of fresh air in a long series of big spenders. But it is not enough to make adjustments in the economy as a whole, or even government spending as a whole. These steps must be complemented with an aggresive program to provide incentives for efficiency and frugality in the federal bureaucracy—and to take away the rewards for bigness and increased spending. The managers who make the real decision whether money is spent efficiently or not must be given the incentive to save money and return it to the public coffers."

This "quote" comes from the book *The Destiny of America.* Leichtman is just warming up. Franklin D. Roosevelt comes onstage a few pages later, sounding like the chairman of the Republican party. Here are some excerpts:

"There are two problems with Social Security. The first is that it has become something it was never intended to be. It was never intended to provide the sole support of a retired individual. . . . There are only two alternatives for overhauling the Social Security system: either up the tax or cut the benefits. It's very simple. . . .

"Of course, in my day we had different ideas about the policy of America. But they were for a different time and a different set of problems. That does not mean that they were bad ideas, but they are pretty worn out today. And I would be the first to say that the New Deal is now the Old Deal, and we need a better deal today. [Laughter.]

"Of course," Leichtman's Roosevelt continues, "there are still some worn-out politicians who hang on to the ideas we had in those days as though they were gospel. They are still entrenched in the old rhetoric. Now, those ideas and economic policies were fine for that time. They worked and we're proud of that. But now it's clear that those same ideas won't work anymore. We need to find some new ones. We need to bring the pendulum back, to fiscal responsibility, cut the deficits, not borrow so much, and be more prudent. . . . Borrowing continually is the road to bankrupcy. And if we continue acting as we have been, we are going to go bankrupt—and that will be a helluva mess."

LEICHTMAN: Well, at present, we are still a very
     powerful and wealthy country.
ROOSEVELT: A very powerful and wealthy country
     heading for bankruptcy. . . . I think it's refresh-
     ing that we have a new president in the White
     House [Reagan] saying, "Let's try some new
     ideas. Of course, the old idea people are ranting
     and raving, 'You can't do this. You can't take all
     this away from us. And I say, 'To heck with
     them.' "

To me, this doesn't sound a heck of a lot—or even a helluva lot—like Roosevelt, alive or dead.

To press on to Mark Twain, one of the problems with

Leichtman's version is that "Twain" never says anything funny, although the "[Laughter]"'s are spread though the text with wild abandon. This caper was done when Jimmy Carter was still in the White House. Here is a passage:

LEICHTMAN: John Kennedy had a good sense of humor.

TWAIN: Kennedy had an excellent sense of humor, and had some friends up here who were helping him, too—and that was very important. The president who is currently in office [in 1980], however, has almost none.

LEICHTMAN: He does have a funny brother, though. [Laughter.]

TWAIN: A funny brother and a funny smile, but very little humor. Of course, the administration is so laughable that further humor is probably unnecessary. [More laughter.]

LEICHTMAN: That's true.

Will Rogers steps into the interview for a few pages, and he isn't funny either. An excerpt:

ROGERS: We have a club up here and we all get together and make up new jokes. Of course, there's never a lack of material. All you have to do is look around you.

JAPIKSE [one of Leichtman's associates]: So what is the latest joke in heaven?

ROGERS: The latest joke in heaven?

JAPIKSE: Yes.

ROGERS: Well, the latest joke in heaven is that you are asking this question. [Laughter.]

Leichtman has the spirit of Abraham Lincoln worried sick about the plight of the rich and successful. He quotes Lincoln, who throughout the book devoted to him seems to have mislaid the wit that distinguished him in life, as follows:

LINCOLN: The successful people of the country are *not* running for office because of the humiliation elected officials must now undergo, being grilled on how nasty and underhanded they were in the way they made their money. And then there is the problem that even if they are elected they will be envied, not respected, by large segments of the populace because they have been successful. The envy of wealth in this country today is a terrible problem. And so the average successful business person or lawyer or other public-minded individual simply will not expose himself or herself to this humiliation.

With Shakespeare, Leichtman gets into some antic exchanges:

LEICHTMAN: Would you like some questions, then?

SHAKESPEARE: Oh, whatever.

LEICHTMAN: Well, I could begin in various places. Let me see what I have here. Do you want the heavy stuff now or the light stuff?

SHAKESPEARE: Oh, suit yourself. Since you've already gotten into the heavy stuff . . .

LEICHTMAN: Ha!

SHAKESPEARE: No fair hitting a spook!

Shakespeare seems to have made a remarkable adjustment from Elizabethan speech to late twentieth-century American idiom. But possibly he keeps an ear open up there.

Later in the Shakespeare book, I found a rather unexpected passage:

SHAKESPEARE: Many of the plays played considerably longer than the versions you have of them now. Depending on the conditions and temper of the audience, sometimes we would extend them, sometimes shorten them.

LEICHTMAN: Fancy that.

SHAKESPEARE: Theater in those days was very rough and ready. [Laughter.]

LEICHTMAN: And of course you weren't forced to stop so the popcorn vendor could make his pennies.

SHAKESPEARE: Well, we had orange vendors, and sweetmeat vendors . . . and sweet skin vendors. [Much laughter.] The actors did have to compete with *those* people, and they were more of a problem than popcorn vendors are nowadays. I remember that on numerous occasions we were inundated with ladies of the evening who were so noisy that the actors could not be heard. Of course, this was part of the fun of going to the theater in those days. And there were also times when some of the ladies on stage would be hawking their wares. This is why, incidentally, we would frequently cast a boy in a female role. At least it kept things in some kind of perspective. Actresses often got carried away. As I understand it, they still do sometimes.

This was a revelation to me; as an English major in college many years ago, I was told that *no* women appeared on the Elizabethan stage. Aquiver with this new information, I sought expert testimony. I live in Boston, and the streets here are practically paved with expert testimony; that is if you include Cambridge across the river, home of those renowned bastions of left-brain thinking, Harvard and the Massachusetts Institute of Technology. I chose Harvard on this one, and was referred to G. Blakemore Evans. He is a retired professor who was textual editor of the *Riverside Shakespeare*, considered the most authoritative present-day collection of Shakespeare's works. Blakemore told me in no uncertain terms that *no* actresses appeared on the Elizabethan stage. I didn't dare tell him where I had gotten the idea that they might have. Harvard authorities might pass the word to hang up, or better yet, call the police, if I called again.

Forbes, the business magazine, recently ran an article entitled "Mainstream Metaphysics." The article appeared in a section headed "Marketing," and was headed by this explanatory note:

"The baby boom generation is big on spiritual and self-awareness. How do you use this fad to sell everday products?"

Now if that isn't as American as apple pie, I don't know what is. Sort of gives you a lump in the throat. Spirituality has really made it in this country when they start figuring how to make big bucks on it.

One of the spearheads of this inspiring new thrust is Michael Goodrich, a former advertising salesman, who has been acting as agent for psychics in the New York area. He calls his outfit Cosmic Consciousness—as in

"Spirits are soaring at Cosmic Consciousness."

The stars of Goodrich's stable are Bill Kase and Rock Nelson.

They are gushers—in conversation, at least.

"The media," says Kase, "has made Rock and me the second most famous channelers in the country, Ramtha still being the first, I think."

(Ramtha purports to be an ancient Hindu god-man who lived thirty-five-thousand years ago and who now speaks through a Seattle woman named J. Z. Knight. He enjoyed great popularity in recent years among the faithful, but has said a lot of strange things lately and had lost a portion of his supporters, including Shirley MacLaine.)

Bill says, "We're in *Omni* magazine now; we're in *Figaro Madame,* a French magazine. We've been in *People* magazine, in *Elle.*"

Rock joins in: "Actually, we're the most active psychics in the world right now. We're on Japanese television, we're on TV or radio practically every other day."

"They're crazed," says Goodrich, meaning they are busy.

They teach nine or ten courses every month, and give private readings at one hundred dollars an hour.

An article in *People* magazine tells us:

"At the last two [readings] Kase has become the vessel for the spirits of a Ming dynasty Chinese lord and Sir Arthur Conan Doyle. Elsewhere, Kenyon has done a séance for *Spin* magazine with dead rock personalities. Although details of that session are officially embargoed, Goodrich can reveal that Elvis put in an appearance. ('He didn't say much. He's still pretty screwed up.') and that Brian Epstein, the Beatles' late manager, is still angry with them."

Rock Kenyon
(Photo © 1986 by John Kenney)

Bill Kase
(Photo © 1986 by John Kenney)

I spoke with the author of the article, David H. Van Biema. In view of the underlying tone of his story, I don't think I'm violating a confidence to reveal that Van Biema has the same conception of Goodrich, et al, that Justin Kaplan has of Elwood Babbitt, although Van Biema couched his assessment in less colorful terms.

Goodrich provided me with Kase's and Kenyon's phone number. Kase answered and hit the ground running.

"We just did a show for NBC News, and JFK and Lindbergh came through. Channeling is the hot thing now. There's a statue outside the Federal Building here of George Washington. It's on Rock's hauntings tour. We did it on Japanese television. There's an interesting aura that shows up on photographs that have been taken of this statue. Washington tends to come through Rock. The Washington Monument also shows a definite aura around it."

Rock told me that the late Frank Lloyd Wright, architect of the Guggenheim Museum in New York, has been around the museum of late. A controversy had boiled up concerning changes in the museum, and has received considerable local media coverage. According to Rock, Wright wants things left as they are. I called the museum, but they denied knowledge of any haunting incidents. They suggested that I call Taliesin, a school of architecture in Scottsdale, Arizona, dedicated to the concepts of the famed architect. I asked if there had been any evidence of Wright's spirit around there lately. The lady who answered said no and seemed oddly eager to get off the phone.

But then again, Rock and Bill weren't at either of

those places; they were in a TV studio, where they have a weekly program on cable TV called "The Psychic Revolution."

"We do three or four shows at a time," Rock told me. They sit in the studio, and whammo, all those big-name spooks come through! Edison, Washington, Galileo, Whitman . . . the mind reels!

"I think it's pretty exciting," says Rock.

Sources

Chapter 1: Are Gable and Lombard Haunting This Little Hotel in Arizona?

Personal interviews with Doris Acres, Ken Keene, Kenny Kingston, Dolly Miller, and Billie Jo Trammel.
Articles in the *Globe,* the *National Enquirer,* and the *Sun.*

Chapter 2: Judy Garland and the Runway Lightbulb

Personal interviews with Larry Davies and Lynn Gardner.
Obituary for Judy Garland in the *New York Times,* June 23, 1969.

Chapter 3: Was That John Hodiak Looking in the Window?

Personal interviews with Hal Gefsky and Kenny Kingston.
Kingston, Kenny. *Psychic Kenny Kingston's Guide to Health and Happiness.*

Chapter 4: Ida Lupino Gets a Ghostly Phone Call

Personal interview with D. Scott Rogo.
Fate, Aug. 1962.
Walker, Danton. *Spooks Deluxe* (New York: Taplinger, 1956).

Chapter 5: Audrey Meadows and Her Nice Ghost

Kleiner, Dick. *Fate*, Jan. 1964.

Chapter 6: What Marilyn Monroe Wants Known

Personal interviews with Kenny Kingston and Walter Uphoff.
Documents furnished by Walter Uphoff.
Barbanell, Maurice. *He Walks in Two Worlds*.

Chapter 7: Elke Sommer's Scary House

Personal interviews with Brenda Crenshaw, James Crenshaw,
Dennis Eisenberg, Jayne Eisenberg, Joe Hyams, and Thelma
Moss.
Crenshaw, James. "Many Saw the Ghost—But She Saw Fire,"
Fate, 1967.
Hyams, Joe. "Haunted." *Saturday Evening Post*, July 2, 1966.
Hyams, Joe. "The Day I Gave Up the Ghost." *Saturday
Evening Post*, June 3, 1967.
Moss, Thelma, and Gertrude R. Schmeidler. "Quantitative
Investigation of a 'Haunted House' with Sensitives and a
Control Group." *Journal of the American Society of Psychical
Research*, 1968.
Transcript of KCOP interview with Diahn Williams.

**Chapter 8: Clifton Webb Just Doesn't
Like Women Sitting in His Chair**

Personal interviews with Kenny Kingston and Richard Senate.
Kingston, Kenny. *Psychic Kenny Kingston's Guide to Health
and Happiness*.

**Chapter 9: In Her Next Incarnation,
Mae West Plans to Get It Right**

Personal interview with Kenny Kingston.
Kingston, Kenny. *Psychic Kenny Kingston's Guide to Health
and Happiness*.
Shaw, Brenda. *Fate*, Jan. 1977.
Shaw, Brenda. *Fate*, April 1977.
Walker, Danton. *Spooks Deluxe* (New York: Taplinger, 1956).

Chapter 10: Dick Clark's Psychic Experience

Personal interviews with Allan Handleman of radio station WPTF, Raleigh, NC; and Dick Clark's secretary.
National Enquirer, Dec. 3, 1985.

Chapter 11: Did Houdini Come Back to Say Hello to His Widow?

Personal interviews with William Rauscher, Allen Spraggett, and Walter Uphoff.
Christopher, Milbourne. *Mediums, Mystics, and the Occult* (New York: Crowell, 1975).
Rauscher, Reverend Canon William V. *The Spiritual Frontier.*
Spraggett, Allen, with William V. Rauscher. *Arthur Ford: The Man Who Talked with the Dead* (New York: New American Library, 1973).
Uphoff, Walter and Mary Jo. *New Psychic Frontiers: Your Key to New Worlds* (Gerrards Cross, Eng.: C. Smythe, 1977).
Uphoff, Walter and Mary Jo, eds. *New Frontiers Center Newsletter*, Spring/Summer 1986.

Chapter 12: John Lennon Doesn't Seem to Have Left

Personal interviews with Linda Deer Domnitz, Bill Harry, Eugenia Macer-Story, Katie MacPherson, Shawn Robbins, Bill Tenuto, and an employee at the Dakota.
Coleman, Ray. *Lennon* (New York: McGraw-Hill, 1984).
Domnitz, Linda Deer. *John Lennon Conversations* (New York: Coleman Publishing Inc., 1984).
Green, John. *Dakota Days: The Untold Story of John Lennon's Final Years* (New York: St. Martin's Press, 1984).
Macer-Story, Eugenia. Poem from the *Woodstock Times*.
McCabe, Peter, and Robert Schonfeld. *John Lennon for the Record* (New York: Bantam, 1984).
Schaffner, Nicholas, and Peter Shotton. *John Lennon in My Life* (New York: Stein and Day, 1983).
Crenshaw, James. "Psychic Adventure in Beverly Hills." *Fate*, April 1987.
"An Interview with John Lennon." *Psychic Guide*, Sept./Oct./Nov. 1983.

Chapter 13: Is That Molière Hanging About in the Wings?

Personal interview with Albert Bermel and Eugenia Macer-Story.
Encyclopaedia Britannica (Chicago: Encyclopaedia Britannica Inc., 1987) and *Concise Oxford Dictionary of French Literature* (New York: Oxford University Press, 1985).

Chapter 14: Monkeys in the Closet (Beatrice Straight)

Personal interview with Beatrice Straight.

Chapter 15: The Spirit of Lee Strasberg Visits His Granddaughter

Personal interview with Susan Strasberg.
Current Biography (New York: H. W. Wilson Co., 1958 and 1960).
Various newspaper accounts.

Chapter 16: The Wild and Crazy Lady Who Haunted Susan Strasberg's House

Personal interview with Susan Strasberg.

Chapter 17: She Felt a Ghost—And It Hurt!

Personal interviews with Joyce M. Caffey and Marie.

Chapter 18: Jimmy and Rosalynn Carter's Haunted House

Cook, Jacquelyn. "Rosalynn Carter's Haunted House." *Good Housekeeping*, May 1979.

Chapter 19: Did Mamie Eisenhower's Ghost Head Off a Parking Lot in Her Backyard?

Personal interviews with Priscilla Baker, Anne Gehman, and a park ranger at the Gettysburg Battlefield.
Courier, Oct. 1986.

Chapter 20: Mackenzie King, Canada's Famed Prime Minister—Or, How to Run a Country and Still Have Time for the Next World

Personal interviews with Don Brittain, Curtis Fuller, J. E. Handy, Bruce Hutchison, Victor Mackie, Jack Pickersgill, A. Edgar Ritchie, and personnel at Laurier House and the Mackenzie King Estate.

Boone, Mike. "King Returns from the Grave," *Toronto Globe and Mail.*

Fodor, Nandor. *They Knew the Unknown.*

Fraser, Blair. "The Secret Life of Mackenzie King, Spiritualist." *Maclean's,* Dec. 15, 1951.

Hutchinson, Bruce. *The Incredible Canaduian.*

Philip, Percy J. "I Talked with Mackenzie King's Ghost." *Fate,* Oct. 1955.

Stacey, C. P. *A Very Double Life: The Private World of MacKenzie King.*

Current Biography (New York: H. W. Wilson Co., 1940).

Dictionary of National Biography: Concise Dictionary, Part 2 (New York: Oxford University Press, Inc., 1982).

McGraw-Hill Encyclopedia of World Biography (New York: McGraw-Hill).

Chapter 21: Does Lincoln's Ghost Still Haunt the White House? Queen Wilhelmina, Winston Churchill, and Reagan's Dog Rex Have Thought So

Personal interview with Priscilla Baker.

Alexander, John. *Ghosts: Washington's Most Famous Ghost Stories* (Washington D.C.: Washington Book Trading Co., 1987).

Fodor, Nandor, ed. *Encyclopedia of Psychic Science.* (Detroit: Gale Research Co., 1984).

Hertz, Emanuel. *The Hidden Lincoln, from Letters and Papers of William H. Herndon* (New York: Viking, 1938).

New York Times, Feb. 13, 1987.

Chapter 22: Belita Adair—Her First Piano Teacher, She Says, Was Beethoven

Personal interviews with Belita Adair, Stephanie Adair, Earl Blew, and James Crenshaw.
Notes furnished by James Crenshaw.
Crenshaw, James and Brenda. *Fate*, May 1979.

Chapter 23: Belita Adair and Elvis Presley

Personal interviews with Belita Adair, Stephanie Adair, George Arnold, and James Crenshaw.
Notes furnished by James Crenshaw.

Chapter 24: Rosemary Brown and Liszt—As Well as Chopin, Beethoven, Bach, Brahms, and Other Friends

Personal interviews with Basil Ramsey, Stewart Robb, and Peggy Williams.
Brown, Rosemary. *Immortals by My Side* (Chicago: Henry Regnery Co., 1975).
Brown, Rosemary. *Unfinished Symphonies* (W. Morrow, 1971).
Fate, May 1971.
Kolodin, Irving. "Rosemary's Babies." *Saturday Review*, Oct. 31, 1970.
Roberts, Charles. "A Presidential Ghost Story." *Newsweek*, Jan. 11, 1971.
"The Voices of Silence." *Time*, July 6, 1970.

Chapter 25: Rosemary Brown and the Composer Who Died in a Concentration Camp

Personal interviews with Basil Ramsey and Stewart Robb.
"Music from Beyond," audiocassette.
Transcript of Bill Jenkins's interview with Kerry Woodward on KABC radio, Los Angeles.
Rosemary Brown's music can be obtained from Basil Ramsey, Publisher of Music, Inc., 1012 Fair Oaks, Suite 230, South Pasadena, CA 91030

Chapter 26: F. W. Woolworth May Not Have Been Your Usual American Business Tycoon

Personal interviews with Martin Carey, Glenn Giwojna, Raymond Graham, Monica Randall, Dan Russell, Frances Tucciardo, and various Pall Corporation employees.

Assistance from Glen Cove Public Library and Hofstra University Library Department of Special Collections.

Brough, James. *The Woolworths* (New York: McGraw-Hill, 1982).

Heymann, C. David. *Poor Little Rich Girl: The Life and Legend of Barbara Hutton* (Secaucus, NJ: L. Stuart Inc., 1984).

Randall, Monica. *The Mansions of Long Island's Gold Coast* (New York: Hastings, 1979).

Winkler, John K. *Five and Ten: The Fabulous Life of F. W. Woolworth* (Salem, NH: Ayer Publishing Co., 1940).

Dictionary of American Biography (New York: Scribner).

Obituary for F. W. Woolworth. *New York Times*, April 9, 1919.

Chapter 27: The Return of the Man Who Invented Florida— Along with a Few Friends and Relatives

Personal interviews with Maxine Banish, Lynn Gardner, Phyllis Guy, Kenneth Jones, and Charles Simmons.

Brochure of the Henry Morrison Flagler Museum.

Various newspaper accounts.

Chapter 28: Allen Ginsberg Hears a Voice

Personal interview with Bob Rosenthal, assistant to Allen Ginsberg.

"Allen Ginsberg." *Paris Review* No. 37, Summer 1966.

Talking Poetics from Naropa Institute: Annals of the Jack Kerouac School of Disembodied Poetics (Boston: Shambhala Publications Inc., 1979).

Chapter 29: Arthur Koestler and the Ghost of His Hostess's Deranged Uncle

Ebon, Martin. "Arthur Koestler's Psychic World." *Fate*, Aug. 1978.

Koestler, Arthur. *Bricks to Babel* (New York: Random House, 1980).
Contemporary Authors (Detroit: Gale Research Co., 1983).
Current Biography (New York: H. W. Wilson Co., 1962).
Obituary for Arthur Koestler in the *New York Times*, March 4, 1983.

Chapter 30: Thomas Wolfe Sprang from Psychic Roots— His Family Could See the Future

Hancock, M. A. "The Psychic Heritage of Thomas Wolfe." *Fate*, May 1981.
Twentieth Century Authors: A Biographical Dictionary of Modern Literature (New York: H. W. Wilson Co., 1955).

Chapter 31: Does the Ghost of Elinor Wylie Haunt the MacDowell Colony?

Personal interviews with John Fuller, Susan Moody, and MacDowell Colony administrators.
Fuller, John. *The Ghost of Flight 401* (New York: Berkley Pub. Corp., 1976).

Chapter 32: Admiral Byrd and His Granddaughter

Personal interviews with Bolling Clarke and Evelyn Clarke.
Byrd, Richard Evelyn. *Alone* (New York: Avon, 1981), originally published 1938.
Current Biography (New York: H. W. Wilson Co., 1942 and 1956).
Obituary for Admiral Byrd in the *New York Times*, March 12, 1957.

Chapter 33: Who Goes There? Could It Be Buffalo Bill Cody?

Personal interview with Joyce Elliott.
Alexander, John. *Ghosts: Washington's Most Famous Ghost Stories* (Washington, D.C.: Washington Book Trading Co., 1987).
Blueprints, the magazine of the National Building Museum.
National Building Museum brochure.

Chapter 34: There Goes Crazy Horse—Sitting Bull Went Thataway—and Custer's Just over the Hill

Rickey, Don, and Neil C. Mangum. *Courier*, Oct. 1986.

Chapter 35: "I've Seen Spirits of the Dead— Twice," Says Dr. Christiaan Barnard

Personal interview with staff member of Baptist Medical Center's Transplantation Institute.
National Enquirer, Sept. 3, 1985.

Chapter 36: Carl Gustav Jung—Scientist and Mystic

Adler, Gerhard. *Selected Letters of C. J. Jung, 1909–1961* (Princeton, NJ: Princeton University Press, 1984).
Brome, Vincent. *Jung* (New York: Atheneum, 1978).
Hannah, Barbara. *Jung, His Life and Work: A Biographical Memoir* (New York: Putnam, 1976).
Jaffe, Aniela. *Apparitions and Precognition* (Dallas: Spring Publications).
Jung, C. G. *Memories, Dreams, Reflections* (Pantheon, 1963).
Mattoon, Mary Ann. *Jungian Psychology in Perspective* (New York: Free Press, 1981).
Von Franz, Marie-Louise. *C. J. Jung: His Myth in Our Time* (New York: Putnam, 1975).
Encyclopaedia Britannica (Chicago: Encyclopaedia Britannica Inc., 1987).
Encyclopedia Americana (Danbury, CT: Grolier Inc., 1987).
Collier's Encyclopedia.

Chapter 37: Norman Vincent Peale and His Mystical Experiences

Peale, Norman Vincent. *The True Joy of Positive Living* (New York: Morrow, 1984).
Letter from Norman Vincent Peale.

Chapter 38: Voices of the Dead on Tape?
Sadat, Ben Franklin, Carl Jung, Hitler

Personal interviews with Sarah Estep, founder of the American Association–Electronic Voice Phenomena, 726 Dill Road, Severna Park, MD 21146.

Bander, Peter. *Voices from the Tapes* (New York: Drake Publishers, 1973).

Raudive, Konstantin. *Breakthrough: An Amazing Experiment in Electronic Communication with the Dead* (New York: Taplinger, 1971).

Rogo, D. Scott, and Raymond Bayless. *Phone calls from the Dead* (Englewood Cliffs, NJ: Prentice-Hall, 1979).

Stemman, Roy. *Spirits and Spirit Worlds* (New York: Danbury Press, 1975).

Uphoff, Walter and Mary Jo. *New Psychic Frontiers: Your Key to New Worlds* (Gerrards Cross, Eng.: C. Smythe, 1977).

Material furnished by Walter Uphoff, New Frontiers Center, Route #1, Oregon, WI 53575.

Chapter 39: Celebrities Galore—They're Pouring Down Through the Channelers!

Personal interviews with G. Blakemore Evans, Anne Gehman, Michael Goodrich, Justin Kaplan, Bill Kase, Rock Kenyon, Robert R. Leichtman, Roger Pile, David H. Van Biema, and Paul Zuromski.

Leichtman, Robert. *Destiny of America* (Columbus, OH: Ariel Press, 1984).

Leichtman, Robert. *Lincoln Returns* (Columbus, OH: Ariel Press, 1983).

Leichtman, Robert. *Mark Twain Returns* (Columbus, OH: Ariel Press, 1982).

Leichtman, Robert. *Shakespeare Returns* (Columbus, OH: Ariel Press, 1978).

Psychic Guide, June/July/Aug., 1983.

Trachtenberg, Jeffrey A., and Edward Giltenan. "Mainstream Metaphysics." *Forbes*, June 1, 1987.

Van Bieman, David H. "For Those Who See the Past and the Future, But Can't Find Their Way to the Bank, Michael Goodrich Offers—Himself." *People*, May 18, 1987.

Fate, May, June, July, August 1987.